John Townley

Astrological
Life Cycles
A
A Planetary Guide to
Personal & Career Opportunities

by John Townley

illustrated by Barbara Samuels

Destiny Books
Rochester, Vermont

To my father, who always wanted me to have a career . . .

Destiny Books
One Park Street
Rochester, Vermont 05767

Library of Congress Cataloging-in-Publication Data

Townley, John, 1945-
  Astrological life cycles.

  Rev. ed. of: New age career cycles. c1980.
  1. Astrology. 2. Cycles—Miscellanea. I. Townley,
John, 1945-   . New age career cycles. II. Title.
BF1725.T68 1987   133.5   87-13712
ISBN 0-89281-169-2

10 9 8 7 6 5 4 3 2 1

Destiny Books is a division of Inner Traditions International, Ltd.

Printed and bound in the United States

Distributed to the book trade in the United States by Harper & Row Publishers, Inc.
Distributed to the book trade in Canada by Book Center, Inc., Montreal, Quebec

CONTENTS

INTRODUCTION

When an important decision about your income or your career has to be made, do you know the best time to do it?

Do you know when it's better to insist on a personal job interview rather than send a resume? And do you know when a resume alone will do you more good?

Do you know the *right* time to ask for a raise or a job transfer? And also the time when asking for one could bring your career to a dead halt?

Do you know which of your colleagues simply cannot help but boost your career and which will spell disaster to your efforts, *without even knowing it?*

Do you know what times in your life others will be looking to you for new ideas, and when you will be expected to toe the establishment line?

All of these things are profoundly influenced—some say determined—by natural cycles, like intertwining tides that ebb and flow through and around all of us. If you know when to catch the outflowing tide, it can carry you to a sea of success. If you don't, you could get washed up for good in the backwaters of frustration and failure.

Most people struggle through life without ever knowing just why things seem to go for or against them. Some individuals toil ceaselessly without ever reaping a reward, while others, who don't seem to deserve it, are swept to the heights of fortune

Knowledge is power—and knowing the natural cycles gives you the power to use them to your advantage. Cycles are not destiny, but simply a natural phenomenon. If you know the forces surrounding you, you can employ your willpower to use them or to overcome them. No amount of willpower will help you if you are ignorantly battling the tides of man and nature. Millions of ambitious and talented people are forced to accept failure for this reason—and they never know why.

This book will give you some of the critical keys of knowledge that permit you to control your situation instead of being controlled by it. It will also tell you when to be still and do nothing until the time is right. It provides you with such information as:

- Your yearly highs and lows in personal energy and how to use them.
- Your personal image as others see you—how it changes without your knowing it.
- Your natural "friends" and "enemies": people who will help or hurt you and how to spot them.
- Times of personal trial or testing—and how to pass them with flying colors.
- Your lifetime career potential—how you can use it to pick a career, expand a career, or change careers.
- Your peak success cycles—and how to make the most of them.

Knowledge of these basic life and career cycles can make all the difference between a life of pointless struggle and one of creative success.

Don't be a pawn of fate, blaming what you can't understand or control on ill destiny or bad luck.

Hitch yourself to a star—and let the knowledge of the natural cycles surrounding you carry you on to success.

CYCLES THAT CONTROL YOUR LIFE

For thousands of years it's been believed that the fortunes of men and women move in cycles. The ancients depicted the concept as the great Wheel of Fortune, eternally turning and spilling off the winners on top while bearing up the wretches beneath and giving them their time in the limelight before they, too, get dumped. The trouble was that no one knew for sure what powered that wheel or exactly what speed it was turning for any given individual. People knew their days were numbered, but they didn't know the number.

Until recently the situation hasn't improved much. For hundreds of years we have known that it is the regular and predictable cycles of the moon and sun that regulate the ocean's tides, but the tides in the affairs of men have not been so easily forecast. It was almost as if they moved erratically of their own accord, unmotivated by outside forces.

The extensive cycle research of the past thirty years has proved otherwise. It has established numerous links between regularly occurring human behavior and external natural cycles ranging from weather and solar radiation to phases of the moon and planetary cycles. Here are some dramatic examples.

Murder Tides

At the University of Miami psychologist Arnold Lieber and his colleagues decided to test the old belief of full-moon "lunacy," which most scientists had written off as an old wives' tale. The researchers collected data on homicide in Dade County (Miami) over a period of 15 years—1,887 murders, to be exact. When they matched the incidence of homicide with the phases of the moon, they found, much to their surprise, that the two rose and fell together, almost infallibly, for the entire 15 years! As the full or the new moon approached, the murder rate rose sharply; it distinctly declined during the first and last quarters of the moon.

In order to find out if this was just a statistical fluke, the researchers repeated the experiment using murder data from Cuyahoga County in Ohio (Cleveland). Again, the statistics showed that more murders do indeed occur at the full and new moons.

Dr. Lieber and his colleagues shouldn't have been so surprised. An earlier report by the American Institute of Medical Climatology to the Philadelphia Police Department entitled *The Effect of the Full Moon on Human Behavior* found similar results. That report showed that the full moon marks a monthly peak in various kinds of psychotically oriented crimes such as murder, arson, dangerous driving, and kleptomania. People do seem to get a little bit crazier about that time of the month.

That's something most police and hospital workers have known for a long time. Indeed, back in eighteenth-century England, a murderer could plead "lunacy" if he committed his crime during the full moon, and get a lighter sentence as a result.

Scientists, however, like to have a hard physical model to explain their discoveries, and so far there isn't one. Dr. Lieber speculates that perhaps the human body, which, like the surface of the earth, is composed of almost 80 percent water, experiences some kind of "biological tides" that affect the emotions. When a person is already on psychologically shaky ground, such a "biological tide" can push him over the edge.

Bloody Moon

Crimes and violence aren't the only things affected by the 29½-day full-moon cycle. In the *Journal of the Florida Medical Association*, Dr. Edson J. Andrews writes that in a study of 1,000 tonsillectomies 82 percent of postoperative bleeding crises occurred nearer the full than the new moon—despite the fact that fewer operations were performed at that time! Clearly, the full moon is a dangerous time for surgery, and the dissemination of this knowledge should result in planning operations for the new moon.

Moon Dollars

Practical economic use of the lunar cycle has been going on for a long time. In tropical rain forest countries in South America and Southeast Asia, where most of the world's hardwood comes from, tree-harvesting contracts are linked to the phase of the moon. The trees are only cut down on a waning moon, as near to the new moon as feasible. This is because on a waxing or full moon, the sap rises in the trees and extensive sap bleeding attracts hordes of deathwatch beetles, which will devastate a crop. Awareness of this cycle means the difference between making or losing millions of dollars every year.

Lunar Babies

One future use for the monthly lunar cycle may be in choosing the timing and gender of babies. Curtis Jackson, controller of Southern California Methodist Hospital, reports that more babies are conceived on the waxing moon than on the waning. He quantified 11,025 births over a period of 6 years and found that nearly 1,000 more children were conceived during the waxing moon. Apparently, successful conception is easier at that time. More interesting are the results of German researcher W. Buehler. In an analysis of 33,000 births Dr. Buehler found that there was a significant preponderance of male births during the waxing moon. This knowledge, combined

Full-moon madness

with medical techniques known to affect fertility and sex, may well help people in planning for their children.

Harnessing the Solar Wind

The moon isn't the only body out in space that produces human cycles. The sun, the basic source of all life on earth, has its own rhythm, which produces cycles in humans and nonhumans alike. Since the 1800s astronomers have noted that there is an 11- and a 22-year sunspot cycle: that is, for some years there would be hardly any sunspots, and then for some years the sun's face would be as blotchy as a teenager's with acne. It wasn't until the 1930s, however, that it occured to anyone that something going on that far away from earth could affect us. During the sunspot peak of the 1930s Dr. Miki Takata found that human blood serum was affected by the solar radiation put out by sunspots. During the same period it was discovered that sunspot emissions affected a wide variety of ther things, such as the size of tree rings and the amount of radio interference on certain bandwidths.

During World War II the potential communications blackout that sunspots and solar storms might cause was of great concern to the armed forces, so a radio engineer at RCA named John Nelson was asked to come up with a method of predicting when the storms would occur. Nelson figured the only major variables that might conceivably affect the sun's turbulent surface were the planets surrounding it. He devised a system of charting their relationships to the sun and to one another, and found that when certain angular relationships between planets occurred, sunspots and solar magnetic storms broke out. To date, his system of prediction has been 95 percent accurate, and the hypothesis that the planets cause solar "tides" was proved by Professor K.D. Wood at the University of Colorado.

More recently, many scientists have been suggesting that the sunspot cycle is critical in the formation of our weather patterns. Indeed, during a 70-year period in the seventeenth and eighteenth centuries when the cycle was interrupted and sunspots stopped for no apparent reason, Europe was plunged into its coldest period on record, nicknamed the "Little Ice Age." Astronomer John R. Gribben and astrophysicist Stephen H. Plagemann have even gone so far as to suggest that sunspot and planetary cycles are linked to earthquakes, and a coming unusual planetary alignment may trigger a devastating California quake. The more the subject is investigated, the more important these cycles appear.

Mass Hysteria

The amount of solar radiation we receive, which is determined by the sunspot cycle, may have profound historical significance. Soviet professor A.C. Tchyivsky has correlated the 11-year cycle with what he calls a worldwide "mass excitement cycle." He found that throughout history events such as wars, migrations, crusades, uprisings, and revolutions have clustered around peak sunspot periods. In the 3 years surrounding these peaks 60 percent of such events occurred, while only 5 percent occurred in the troughs. It would appear that tides govern the affairs of nations as well as individuals.

Government Cover-up

But can planetary cycles directly affect individual human events? If the answer is yes, then cycle research begins to look pretty much like astrology, a subject most scientists aren't too fond of.

An Atomic Energy Commission-funded project at Sandia Laboratories in Albuquerque, New Mexico, came up with a report entitled *Intriguing Accident Patterns Plotted Against a Background of Natural Environmental Features*, which correlated on-the-job accidents of goverment employees over a period of 20 years with various natural cycles. This preliminary report (the researches suggested further study was in order) found that accidents peak with the sunspot cycle and—even more intriguing and "astrological"—that people were more likely to have accidents during the phase of the moon the same as or opposite to that under which they were born.

Some really hard and startling evidence might have come out of this research had it been allowed to continue. But alas, that was not to be. Shortly after its completion, the report fell into the hands of *Time* magazine, which did a spoof on it in a January 10, 1972, issue, under the heading "Moonstruck Scientists," complete with an old woodcut of maidens dancing in a frenzy under the rays of the full moon.

That was all the Congress needed to kill the project and suppress the report. When I wrote to the Atomic Energy Commission and Sandia in 1972, I was told the report was not for distribution and that I, or any other taxpayer, could not see it. The report remained classified until 1977, when I again requested a copy, this time under the provisions of the Freedom of Information Act. At first, I was told that all extant copies has been lost, but through the efforts of a persistent Energy Research Administration officer, Sandia was finally pressured into coughing up a copy—accompanied by a somewhat terrified disclaimer telling me I really shouldn't believe what was in it.

J.E. Davidson, who with a team of fellow scientists wrote the report, told me over the phone that he was sad the research had been canceled. The team felt they were on to something and, except for a nosy journalist and premature publicity, might have made a significant contribution to cycle research. Instead, their work was thrown down the drain. But that's the breaks when Congress is your boss.

Statistics Don't Lie, Only Statisticians Do

Probably the most distinguished work connecting planetary cycles with events and trends in the lives of individuals has been that of French psychologist and statistician Michel Gauquelin. In the mid-1960s he set out to disprove astrology statistically by analyzing planetary positions at the births of professionals, using samples as large as 10,000, 15,000, and 20,000. Astrologers have always believed that certain planets coming up over the horizon or directly overhead at a person's birth guide that individual toward a certain profession.

To Gauquelin, the task he had set for himself seemed like a piece of cake. All he had to do was prove that the planet associated with athletic achievement, Mars, fell at random points in the nativities of 10,000 or 15,000 athletes, and that would be that— astrology would be debunked. In order to emphasize his point he also investigated

UNITED STATES
ATOMIC ENERGY COMMISSION
WASHINGTON, D.C. 20545

FEB 10 1972

Mr. John W. Townley, Jr.,
Editor, The Astrological Review
520 Fifth Avenue
New York, New York 10036

Dear Mr. Townley:

This is in response to your written inquiry of February 6. There are no copies of the Sandia report "Intriguing Accident Patterns Against a Background of Natural Environmental Features" available at AEC Headquarters. You may be interested in contacting Sandia Laboratories at P. O. Box 5800, Albuquerque, New Mexico 87115. Thank you for your interest.

Sincerely,

Martin Moon
Public Information Officer
Office of Information Services

SANDIA LABORATORIES
SANDIA CORPORATION
ALBUQUERQUE, NEW MEXICO 87115

February 23, 1972

John W. Townley, Jr., Editor
The Astrological Review
520 Fifth Avenue
New York, N. Y. 10036

This is in response to your letter expressing interest in the report entitled Intriguing Accident Patterns Plotted Against a Background of Natural Environment Features.

This report was not intended for general release. Some copies were sent to people who provided input to the report, and one of these reports evidently came to the attention of Time.

The report was a treatment of data which appeared to have correlations with environmental phenomena. Upon closer scrutiny and more scientific treatment of the data, it is now our opinion that the data is inadequate to draw significant conclusions.

We therefore do not intend to further distribute this report.

Yours truly,

L. M. Jercinovic, Manager
Security and Safety Standards
Department - 3510

LMJ/hs

groups of doctors, lawyers, writers, and others in jobs associated with specific planets by astrologers.

To Gauquelin's surprise, the results turned out to be exactly the opposite of what he had expected. Mars *did* appear to be rising or culminating in a vast number of athletes' birth charts. Similarly, Jupiter appeared for bankers, Saturn for doctors, Mercury for writers, and so on. Gauquelin was astounded. Had he accidentally *proved* the case for astrology when he had meant to debunk it?

Actually, he had done a lot more than that because his data not only confirmed traditional astrological assignments, they uncovered new ones. For writers, for instance, the traditionally associated planet is Mercury. Gauquelin found that Mercury was indeed significant in writers' natal charts, but he also found that the moon was equally important, something astrologers had never posited.

Gauquelin's work established the fact that planetary positions do affect human disposition, talent, and direction, and that these effects can be specifically determined by scientific methods such as statistical analysis and probability. His later studies show significant planetary links on a mass scale between parents and children.

The more research that is done on planetary effects, the clearer it becomes that we must rely on observation rather than on mere astrological belief to understand these effects. This is because investigation has so far been finding as much error in traditional astrology as truth. This is only natural, because astrological lore is a mishmash of

Saturn

Mercury and the moon

thousands of years of unorganized observation and varying religious beliefs, none of which is compatible with modern investigative techniques. Traditional astrology may be used as a starting point for investigation, but not as a reliable guidepost. A new set of analytic guidelines is being drawn up determined by concrete observation and logical thought rather than by mystical assumptions or outworn tradition. Two different avenues of investigation are being pursued: the causative and the associative.

Investigation into the physical cause-and-effect link between planetary cycles and human behavior is still in its infancy, but it is growing fast. The connection is likely either gravitational or electromagnetic—probably the latter, according to recent experiments. It has been shown that the manipulation of weak magnetic fields around test animals' brains can seriously affect and sometimes impair learned behavior. The levels used were similar to the weak electromagnetism put out by planetary bodies, so we can surmise that planetary electromagnetism is affecting human beings in a similar, though perhaps not so drastic, manner. The neural or biochemical mechanisms involved have not yet been laid bare; only their existence has been established.

Mars

Jupiter

Furthermore, it is thought that the high hormonal and biochemical activity during the birth trauma may act as a kind of cement, fixing whatever patterns of electromagnetic input were being received at birth. These theories go a long way in explaining phenomena that have been observed, but we do not yet have a full physiological model to rely on.

Techniques of associative investigation—that is, correlating known behavior patterns with planetary cycles—are more developed than causative investigation. Gauquelin was the first to use them, but the field is becoming crowded with researchers, of whom Lieber, Davidson, Nelson, Tchyivsky, Jackson, and Buehler are just a few. There have been attempted correlations of planetary patterns with patterns of suicide, various diseases, sexual behavior, auto accidents, financial cycles, and even dog and cat breeding and showing. As in any field, some studies are better than others; some are quite conclusive and others prove nothing one way or another. It will require many years of research and analysis before a reliable, relatively complete body of knowledge is assembled.

We can, however, begin to use this knowledge, so long as we take care to stick to areas that have been explored with fairly consistent results. The subject of this book is one such area, verified by 17 years of counseling and research on my part, plus the work of other researchers, particularly Gauquelin.

Planetary Cycles and the Life-Crisis Periods

One area that can be correlated with planetary cycles is the psychological life-crisis periods, fairly well agreed upon by most psychiatrists and psychologists and popularized by Gail Sheehy in her best-selling book *Passages*.

If you take the natural cycles of the planets beyond the orbit of earth (the interior ones, Mercury and Venus, appear to move with the sun from our point of view) and graph them so that the peak of their cycles is the natal position and the trough is its opposite, 180° away, you get a graph like Figure 1. This looks a bit confusing at first, but it does show an interesting kind of symmetry. Removing the planets Neptune and Pluto—which never complete a cycle in any person's lifetime, their periods being 164 years and 245 years, respectively—and averaging the rest of the cycles together, you get a much simpler graph, Figure 2.

Figure 2 depicts quite clearly a total of eleven peaks and valleys, of which all but the oldest—which psychologists haven't really studied—coincide with the generally accepted life-crisis periods. They are:

I.   BIRTH AND INFANCY (age 0-3).

A naturally exuberant, outgoing period of freedom and exploration of the newfound world.

II.   EARLY CHILDHOOD (age 3-9).

When the rules and regulations of the world have to be learned and sobering restrictions are laid on the originally free spirit.

III.   LATE CHILDHOOD (age 9-13).

When the rules have been mastered and the world is again a place of wonder and exploration, before the unexpected complications of puberty set in.

IV.   ADOLESCENCE (age 13-21).

The often difficult period of learning a male or female self-image and learning how to shoulder the coming burdens of adulthood while still under parental restrictions.

V.   YOUNG ADULTHOOD (age 21-37).

The first prime of life, when one sets out in high spirits to conquer the world and make a mark on the order of things.

VI.   MIDDLE AGE (age 37-50).

The most serious crisis period, when one realizes one hasn't conquered the world after all and is no longer young. This period forces a radical reshaping of self-image and the adoption of more spiritual and less tangible personal goals.

VII.   FINAL MATURITY (age 50-64).

The second prime of life, when one may continue to achieve and enjoy the fruits of previous accomplishments at the same time. Most people in this period are as high in career standing as they will ever get, having developed certain creative skills and achieved seniority in their field.

VIII.   RETIREMENT (age 65-71).

When working life is over and the specter of death has to be dealt with and integrated into one's life.

IX.   OLD AGE (age 71-75).

When one is glad to be living on "borrowed time" and enjoys each day to the fullest.

X.   SENILITY (age 75-81).

A period of withdrawal from society, sometimes involving actual senility. All one's friends are gone and the world is going on its way without one, which causes depression.

XI.   REBIRTH (age 81+).

A period in which people who manage to survive this long frequently return to the mainstream and start doing things again, barring too great physical impairment.

The last two or three periods are often seriously affected by ill health or may not be reached at all, but the others are generally accepted life cycles that all of us go through to a greater or lesser extent, their intensity often varying with the accidental vagaries of circumstance that may serve to alleviate or accentuate them.

A close correlation of known life cycles with planetary cycles plotted against birth positions indicates that planetary birth positions are significant in shaping personality, particularly in relation to the later planetary cycles. Going one logical step further, what would be found if we applied these same cycles to the birth horizon and overhead positions that Gauquelin found to be so important in career determination? Would a rhythm of career ups and downs, similar to the life-crisis cycles, appear?

The answer is yes. For the overwhelming majority of the hundreds of people I have

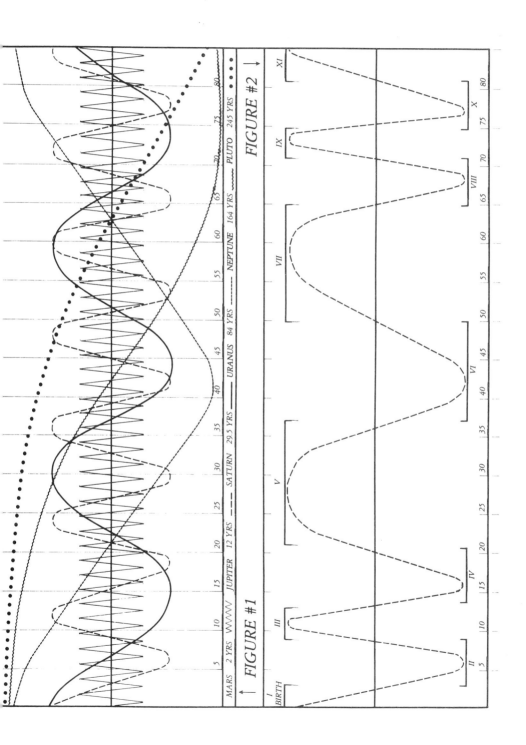

counseled over the past 17 years, career patterns can be depicted quite accurately by applying this technique. In fact, twelve separate cycle determinants can be traced which, when applied to normal planetary cycles, seem to outline not only different facets in the course of a person's career, but also the concomitant learning periods in that person's life that shape reaction to future cycles. Because their effects are sometimes so subjective, repeatable quantification of these cycle periods is a massive and perhaps impossible task to accomplish in the near future. Career learning and personal definitions of success belong more to the realm of psychology than to the field of statistics. But qualification should not prevent us from using what has been discovered to date and testing it by applying it to life situations. So far, in my 17 years of practice as a counselor, I have found that the understanding and conscious use of these cycles have substantially improved the career and life situations of my clients. By observing what external forces are at play, individuals aware of their cycles are able to alter their positions and attitudes so as to take advantage of the flow rather than battle against it. They learn to ride with full tide instead of bucking it.

Unfortunately, most people don't know what these cyclical tides are, when they occur, or how to use them. They swim in an ocean of phenomena they know nothing about, and wonder why things don't seem to turn out right (or, conversely, why they sometimes, quite mysteriously, do). Thus they attribute their successes and failures to good and bad "luck." But there is no such thing as luck, at least as we commonly use the term. What we call luck is simply the operation of forces that are beyond our knowledge.

These forces are what this book is all about. Until now you have probably been unaware of the planetary cycles that are operating on you, creating a lot of "bad luck" and preventing you from exploiting potential "good luck." Now you can observe these cycles and turn them to your advantage. By the time you have finished this book you will realize that many events and trends in your past could have been foreseen and perhaps altered for the better. More important, you will be able to see what's coming up and know how to handle it so that you come out on top, not on the bottom.

Certainly cycles aren't the only unseen factors operating on your life and career, and you won't become 100 percent master of your fate by learning them. But you will find them a significant help, and it would be foolish to ignore them. It's like listening to a weather report—you may not be able to stop it from raining, but you will know enough to carry an umbrella so you can get where you're going without becoming drenched.

There is a lot of information here, and it should be read carefully, not skimmed. If you just pick up bits and pieces or are careless in determining your cycles, you will attain only partial understanding: therefore only partial success. If you take it slowly, step by step, you will gain a distinct advantage in controlling your direction. Like any good tool, this information must be used properly to get the most out of it.

2

THE MONTHLY AND YEARLY CYCLES

The Ascendant

In order to apply planetary cycles to your birth horizon, you must determine what part of the sky was rising over the eastern horizon at the time of your birth. That is a function of not only the day and year of your birth, but also the *time* of the day you were born. Therefore, you must find out the time of your birth to within a few minutes for maximum accuracy, but at least to within 15 to 20 minutes.

If you don't know your birth time, you can obtain this information from the state, town, or hospital in which you were born for a nominal fee. For those born in the United States and its possessions, a list of addresses and fees is here provided.

Once you know the time of day (in *Standard*, not Daylight Savings, Time), just add it to your birthday key number and look up the result, as explained in the section "Finding Your Ascendant." The Ascendant is the part of the sky that was rising on the eastern horizon at the time of your birth, and it is the starting point for most of the cycles discussed in this book, so it is very important to get it right. Double-check this; once you're certain of it, the rest is easy.

HOW TO OBTAIN BIRTH TIME INFORMATION

If you are serious about career cycles, it is worth your while to find out your birth time as accurately as possible. Parents' memories are often unreliable. Unless your birth time was written down in family records—a baby book, for example—the first place to look for it is your birth certificate. To help you obtain a copy of your birth certificate, we have taken information concerning birth records from the U.S. government pamphlet entitled **Where to Write for Birth and Death Records,** with the permission of the Department of Health, Education, and Welfare. In a few cases where the information in that pamphlet was out of date, we have corrected it.

When you write for your birth certificate, tell the agency you are writing because you want to know your birth time. If they have it on record, they will send you a copy of the birth certificate form that includes it. Some vital records agencies have birth times recorded only in a special medical information section, which is confidential by law. If that is the case, you may not be able to obtain birth-time information for anyone but yourself or your child.

Some vital records agencies did not record birth times at all during some years. In preparing this booklet, we surveyed all sixty agencies listed in it that have birth records for this century and asked them what their records contain. Of the fifty-seven that replied, all but three now ask birth attendants to supply birthtimes. If you cannot get your birth time from a vital records agency, you may be able to get it from the hospital where you were born or from the office of the attending physician.

In writing for a certified copy of your birth certificate, it is suggested that a money order or certified check be enclosed since the office cannot refund cash lost in transit. Fees listed are subject to change.

The letter should give the following facts (type or print all names and addresses):

1. Full name of the person whose record is requested.
2. Sex and race.
3. Parents' names, including maiden name of mother.
4. Month, day, and year of birth.
5. Place of birth (city or town, county and state; name of hospital if any).
6. Purpose for which copy is needed.
7. Relationship to person whose record is requested.

Place of Birth	Cost of Birth Form	Address of Vital Statistics Office	Remarks
Alabama	$3.00	Bureau of Vital Statistics State Dept. of Public Health Montgomery, Alabama 36104	Additional copies at same time are $1.00 each. State office has records since January 1, 1908. Fee for special searches is $3.00 per hour.
Alaska	$3.00	Bureau of Vital Statistics Dept. of Health and Welfare Pouch "H" Juneau, Alaska 99801	State office has records since 1913.
American Samoa	$1.00	Office of the Territorial Registrar Government of American Samoa Pago Pago American Samoa 96799	Registrar has records on file since before 1900.
Arizona	$2.00	Division of Vital Records State Department of Health P. O. Box 3887 Phoenix, Arizona 85030	State office has records since July 1, 1910.
Arkansas		Division of Vital Records Arkansas Dept. of Health 4815 West Markham Street Little Rock, Arkansas 72201	State office has records since February 1, 1914.
California	$2.00	Vital Statistics Section State Dept. of Health 410 N Street Sacramento, California 95814	State office has records since July 1, 1905. For records before that date, write to County Recorder in county of event.

Canal Zone	$2.00	Vital Statistics Clerk Canal Zone Government Health Bureau, Box 0 Balboa Heights, Canal Zone	Central office has records since May 1904.
Colorado	$2.00	Records and Statistics Section Colorado Department of Health 4210 East 11th Avenue Denver, Colorado 80220	State office has birth records since 1910. State office also has birth records for some counties for years prior to 1910. $2.00 fee is for search of files and one copy of record if found.
Connecticut	$2.00	Public Health Statistics Section State Dept. of Health 79 Elm Street Hartford, Connecticut 06115	State office has records from 1935 to present.
Delaware	$2.50	Bureau of Vital Statistics Division of Public Health Dept. of Health and Social Services Jesse S. Cooper Memorial Bldg. Dover, Delaware 19901	Central office has records since 1913.
District of Columbia	$1.00	Dept. of Human Resources Vital Records Section Rm. 1022 300 Indiana Avenue, NW Washington, D.C. 20001	Central office has birth records on file beginning with 1881.
Florida	$2.00	Dept. of Health and Rehabilitative Services Division of Health Bureau of Vital Statistics P.O. Box 210 Jacksonville, Florida 32201	The majority of records date from January 1917. (If the exact date is unknown and more than 1 year has to be searched, the fee is $2.00 for the first year searched and $1.00 for each additional year searched up to a maximum of $25.00. Fee includes a copy of the record if found.)
Georgia	$3.00	Vital Records Unit State Dept. of Human Resources Room 217-H 47 Trinity Avenue, SW Atlanta George 30334	The state office has records since January 1, 1919. For records before that date in Atlanta or Savannah, write to the County Health Department in county of birth. Additional copies of same record ordered at same time are $1.00 each.
Guam	$1.00	Office of Vital Statistics Dept. of Public Health and Social Services Government of Guam P.O. Box 3378 Agana, Guam, M.I. 96910	Office has records on file since October 26, 1901.

Hawaii	$2.00	Research and Statistics Office State Dept. of Health P.O. Box 3378 Honolulu, Hawaii 96801	State office has records since July 1909.
Idaho	$2.00	Bureau of Vital Statistics State Dept of Health and Welfare Statehouse Boise, Idaho 83720	State office has records since 1911.
Illinois	$3.00	Division of Vital Records State Dept. of Public Health 535 W. Jefferson Street Springfield, Illinois 62761	State office has records filed since January 1, 1916. For records filed before that date and for copies of state records since January 1, 1916, write to the County Clerk in county of birth. ($3.00 fee is for search of files and one copy of the record if found. Additional copies of the same record ordered at the same time are $2.00 each.)
Indiana	$3.00	Division of Vital Records State Board of Health 1330 West Michigan Street Indianapolis, Indiana 46206	State office has birth records since October 1, 1907, except for 1949, 1950, 1951, and part of 1952. For records before 1907, write to Health Officer in city or county of birth. Additional copies of same record ordered at same time are $1.00 each.
Iowa	$2.00	Division of Records and Statistics State Dept. of Health Lucas Office Bldg. Des Moines, Iowa 50319	State office has records since July 1, 1880.
Kansas	$2.00	Kansas State Dept. of Health and Environment Bureau of Registration and Health Statistics 6700 S. Topeka Avenue Topeka, Kansas 66620	State office has records from July 1, 1911, to 1949 and from 1967 to present. For records before that date, write to County Clerk in county of birth.
Kentucky	$2.00	Office of Vital Statistics State Dept. of Health 275 East Main Street Frankfort, Kentucky 40601	State office has records since January 1, 1911.
Louisiana	$2.00	Office of Vital Records State Dept. of Health P.O. Box 60630 New Orleans, Louisiana 70160	State office has records since 1940. Birth records available for city of New Orleans from 1881.
Maine	$2.00	Office of Vital Records State Dept. of Health and Welfare State House Augusta, Maine 04333	State office has records since 1900. For records before that year, write to the municipality in which you were born.

Maryland	$2.00	Division of Vital Records State Dept. of Health State Office Building 201 West Preston Street P.O. Box 13146 Baltimore, Maryland 21203	State office has records since 1900.
South Dakota	$2.00	Division of Public Health Statistics Joe Foss Office Bldg. State Dept. of Health Pierre, South Dakota 57501	State office has records since 1968 and access to other records for some births before that date. Ask for a search to be made.
Tennessee	$2.00	Division of Vital Statistics State Dept. of Public Health C-3 Cordell Hull Bldg. Nashville, Tennessee 37219	State office has birth records for entire state from January 1, 1914, to 1948, and from 1968 to present.
Texas	$2.00	Bureau of Vital Statistics Texas Dept. of Health Resources 410 East 5th Street Austin, Texas 78701	State office has records from 1917 to present.
Trust Territory of the Pacific Islands	$0.25 plus $0.10 per 100 words	Office of Health, Statistics and Records Dept. of Health Services Trust Territory Headquarters Saipan M.I. 96950	Courts have records since November 21, 1952. Beginning in 1950, a few records for various islands are temporarily filed with the Hawaii Bureau of Vital Statistics.
Utah	$3.00	Division of Vital Statistics Utah State Dept. of Health 554 South Third East Salt Lake City, Utah 84111	State office has records since 1905, except for parts of 1956.
Vermont	$2.00	Secretary of State Montpelier, Vermont 05602	State office has records from 1953 to present.
Virginia	$2.00	Bureau of Vital Records and Health Statistics State Dept. of Health James Madison Bldg. Box 1000 Richmond, Virginia 23208	State office has records from 1912 to present.
Virgin Islands (U.S.) St. Thomas	$2.00	Registrar of Vital Statistics Charlotte Amalie St. Thomas, Virgin Islands 00802	Registrar has birth records on file from July 1, 1906, to present.
Washington	$3.00	Bureau of Vital Statistics Health Services Division Dept. of Social and Health Services P.O. Box 9709 Olympia, Washington 98504	State office has records from July 1, 1907, to 1949 and 1967 to present.
West Virginia	$1.00	Division of Vital Statistics 1800 Washington Street	State office has records since January 1917. For records prior to

			Charleston, West Virginia 25305	that year, write to Clerk of County Court in the county of birth.
Wisconsin	$4.00	Bureau of Health Statistics Wisconsin Division ofHealth P.O. Box 309 Madison, Wisconsin 53701	State office has some records since 1900, except for September 1948 to November 1949.
Wyoming	$2.00	Vital Records Services Division of Health and Medical Services Hathaway Bldg. Cheyenne, Wyoming 82002	State office has records since July 1909.
New York City (all boroughs)	$3.00	Bureau of Records and Statistics Dept. of Health of New York City 125 Worth Street New York, New York 10013	Records on file from July 1932 to present.
North Carolina	$2.00	Dept. of Human Resources Division of Health Services Vital Records Branch P.O. Box 2091 Raleigh, North Carolina 27602	State office has records from October 1, 1913, to present.
North Dakota	$2.00	Division of Vital Records Office of Statistical Services State Dept. of Health Bismarck, North Dakota 58505	State office has some records from July 1, 1908, to present; years 1908 to 1920 are incomplete.
Ohio	$2.00	Division of Vital Statistics Ohio Dept. of Health G-20 Ohio Departments Bldg. 65 S. Front Street Columbus, Ohio 43215	State office has records from 1908 to 1956 and 1967 to present.
Oklahoma	$2.00	Vital Records Section State Dept. of Health Northeast 10th St. & Stonewall P.O. Box 53551 Oklahoma City, Oklahoma 73105	State office has records from October 1908 to present.
Oregon	$3.00	Vital Statistics Section Oregon State Health Division P.O. Box 231 Portland, Oregon 97207	State office has records from 1920 to present. Records from 1920 to 1930 may be incomplete.
Pennsylvania	$2.00	Division of Vital Statistics State Dept. of Health Central Bldg. 101 South Mercer Street P.O. Box 1528 Newcastle, Pennsylvania 16103	State office has records from January 1, 1906, to present.
Puerto Rico	$0.50	Division of Demographic Registry and Vital Statistics Dept. of Health San Juan, Puerto Rico 00908	Central office has records from July 22, 1931, to present.

Rhode Island	$2.00	Division of Vital Statistics State Dept. of Health Room 101 Health Bldg. Davis Street Providence, Rhode Island 02908	State office has records from 1933 to 1956 and from 1961 to present.
South Carolina	$2.00	Division of Vital Records Bureau of Health Measurement S.C. Dept. of Health and Analysis Environmental Control 2600 Bull Street Columbia, South Carolina 29201	State office has records from January 1, 1915, to present.
Massachusetts	$2.00	Registrar of Vital Statistics Rm. 103 McCormack Bldg. 1 Ashburton Place Boston, Massachusetts 02108	State office has records since 1943. For records prior to that year, write to the City or Town Clerk in place of birth.
Michigan	$2.00	Office of Vital and Health Statistics Michigan Dept. of Public Health 3500 North Logan Street Lansing, Michigan 48914	State office has records from 1906 to 1949 and from 1967 to present.
Minnesota	$2.00	Minnesota Dept. of Health Section of Vital Statistics 717 Delaware Street, SE Minneapolis, Minnesota 55440	State office has records since January 1908. Copies of records prior to 1908 may be obtained from Clerk of District Court in county of birth or from the Minneapolis or St. Paul Health Department if you were born in either city.
Mississippi	$2.00	Vital Records Registration Unit State Board of Health P.O. Box 1700 Jackson, Mississippi 39205	State office has records from 1912 to 1948 and from 1968 to present.
Missouri	$1.00	Broadway Office Bldg. Bureau of Vital Records Division of Health State Dept. of Public Health and Welfare Jefferson City, Missouri 65101	State office has records beginning with January 1910. If you were born in St. Louis (city), St. Louis County, or Kansas City before 1910, write to the City or County Health Department; copies of these records are $2.00 each.
Montana	$2.00	Bureau of Records and Statistics State Dept. of Health and Environmental Sciences Helena, Montana 59601	State office has records from 1919 to 1945 and 1967 to present.
Nebraska	$3.00	Bureau of Vital Statistics State Dept. of Health Lincoln Bldg. 1003 "O" Street Lincoln, Nebraska 68508	State office has records from 1912 to present.
Nevada	$2.00	Dept. of Human Resources Division of Health	State office has records since July 1, 1911. For earlier records, write

		Vital Statistics Office of Vital Records Capitol Complex Carson City, Nevada 89710	to County Recorder in county of birth.
New Hampshire	$2.00	Dept. of Health and Welfare Division of Public Health Bureau of Vital Statistics 61 South Spring Street Concord, New Hampshire 03301	State office has records from 1938 to 1948 and from 1968 to present.
New Jersey	$2.00	State Dept. of Health Bureau of Vital Statistics Box 1540 Trenton, New Jersey 08625	State office has records from 1920 to present.
New Mexico	$2.00	State Health Agency New Mexico Vital Records Services P.O. Box 2348 Santa Fe, New Mexico 87503	State office has records from 1930 to present.
New York (except New York City)	$2.00	Bureau of Vital Records New York State Dept. of Health Tower Bldg. Albany, New York 12237	State office has records from 1911 to present. For records prior to 1914 in Albany, Buffalo, and Yonkers, write to Registrar of Vital Statistics in the city of birth. For the rest of the state, except New York City, write to state office.

List compiled and edited by Para Research © Copyright 1978. Adapted and reprinted by permission.

Finding Your Ascendant

Finding your Ascendant is easy. Simply write down the time of day or night you were born *in Standard Time* on a piece of paper in 24-hour notation. That means, for example, that 3 A.M. would be written 3:00, while 3 P.M. would be written 15:00, or "fifteen hundred hours" as they say in the army.

Then look up your birthday in the Key Number Table. Next to it you will find a number, written in hours and minutes. Add that to your birth time. If the result is greater than 24:00, subtract 24:00; otherwise leave it alone.

Finally, look up where your total falls in the appropriate Ascendant Table (according to where you were born) in order to determine the sign of your Ascendant. Simple enough.

Say, for example, a person was born on December 2 at 10:32 A.M. in Cleveland. The key number for December 2 is 4:41. The time and key number are added:

```
Birth time . . . . . . . . . . 10:32
Key number . . . . . . . .  4:41
                            ─────
Total . . . . . . . . . . . . . 15:13
```

Then the proper Ascendant Table is consulted to find the total, 15:13. This falls in between the listed 13:31-15:23, so the Ascendant is Capricorn.

Here's another example, one in which an hour has to be subtracted for Daylight Savings Time. This person was born on August 17, 1945, at 1:57 A.M. in Washington, D.C. That was during the Second World War when the country used what was called War Time, which is the same as Daylight Savings Time. (Since it has been in use, Daylight Savings Time has generally started in the spring on the last Sunday in April or May and ended in the fall on the last Sunday in September or October. But this varies from one locality to another, so check your hometown records to be sure.)

To convert to Standard Time, subtract one hour: the real birth time is 0:57. Then look up the birthday key number, which for August 17 is 21:39, and add them:

    Birth time.......... 0:57
    Key number........21:39

    Total..............22:36

The total, 22:36, falls between 22:28 and 0:48 on the Ascendant Table, so the Ascendant is Cancer.

Here's one more, for October 9 at 4:39 P.M. (Daylight Savings Time) in New York City. The birth time in 24-hour notation is 15:39 (after subtracting an hour), and the key number for October 9 is 1:08.

    Birth time..........15:39
    Key number........ 1:08

    Total..............16:47

The total, 16:47, falls between 15:24 and 16:50 on the Ascendant Table, so the Ascendant is Pisces.

Now find your own Ascendant.

"Don't worry, Mother. It only happens to George when the sun's on his Ascendant."

KEY NUMBER TABLE

Add the key number next to your birthday to your birth time.
Then look up the results in the proper Ascendant Table.

	January h m	February h m	March h m	April h m	May h m	June h m	July h m	August h m	September h m	October h m	November h m	December h m
1	6 40	8 42	10 33	12 35	14 33	16 35	18 34	20 36	22 38	0 36	2 39	4 37
2	6 44	8 46	10 37	12 39	14 37	16 39	18 38	20 40	22 42	0 40	2 43	4 41
3	6 48	8 50	10 41	12 43	14 41	16 43	18 42	20 44	22 46	0 44	2 46	4 45
4	6 52	8 54	10 44	12 47	14 45	16 47	18 45	20 48	22 50	0 48	2 50	4 49
5	6 56	8 58	10 48	12 51	14 49	16 51	18 49	20 52	22 54	0 52	2 54	4 53
6	7 0	9 2	10 52	21 55	14 53	16 55	18 53	20 56	22 58	0 56	2 58	4 57
7	7 4	9 6	10 56	12 59	14 57	16 59	18 57	21 0	23 2	1 0	3 2	5 1
8	7 8	9 10	11 0	13 2	15 1	17 3	19 1	21 3	23 6	1 4	3 6	5 4
9	7 12	9 14	11 4	13 6	15 5	17 7	19 5	21 7	23 10	1 8	3 10	5 8
10	7 16	9 18	11 8	13 10	15 9	17 11	19 9	21 11	23 14	1 12	3 14	5 12
11	7 19	9 22	11 12	13 14	15 13	17 15	19 13	21 15	23 18	1 16	3 18	5 16
12	7 23	9 26	11 16	13 18	15 17	17 19	19 17	21 19	23 21	1 20	3 22	5 20
13	7 27	9 30	11 20	13 22	15 20	17 23	19 21	21 23	23 25	1 24	3 26	5 24
14	7 31	9 34	11 24	13 26	15 24	17 27	19 25	21 27	23 29	1 28	3 30	5 28
15	7 35	9 37	11 28	13 30	15 28	17 31	19 29	21 31	23 33	1 32	3 34	5 32
16	7 39	9 41	11 32	13 34	15 32	17 35	19 33	21 35	23 37	1 36	3 38	5 36
17	7 43	9 45	11 36	13 38	15 36	17 38	19 37	21 39	23 41	1 39	3 42	5 40
18	7 47	9 49	11 40	13 42	15 40	17 42	19 41	21 43	23 45	1 43	3 46	5 44
19	7 51	9 53	11 44	13 46	15 44	17 46	19 45	21 47	23 49	1 47	3 50	5 48
20	7 55	9 57	11 48	13 50	15 48	17 50	19 49	21 51	23 53	1 51	3 54	5 52
21	7 59	10 1	11 52	13 54	15 52	17 54	19 53	21 55	23 57	1 55	3 57	5 56
22	8 3	10 5	11 55	13 58	15 56	17 58	19 56	21 59	0 1	1 59	4 1	6 0
23	8 7	10 9	11 59	14 2	16 0	18 2	20 0	22 3	0 5	2 3	4 5	6 4
24	8 11	10 13	12 3	14 6	16 4	18 6	20 4	22 7	0 9	2 7	4 9	6 8
25	8 15	10 17	12 7	14 10	16 8	18 10	20 8	22 11	0 13	2 11	4 13	6 12
26	8 19	10 21	12 11	14 13	16 12	18 14	20 12	22 14	0 17	2 15	4 17	6 15
27	8 23	10 25	12 15	14 17	16 16	18 18	20 16	22 18	0 21	2 19	4 21	6 19
28	8 27	10 29	12 19	14 21	16 20	18 22	20 20	22 22	0 25	2 23	4 25	6 23
29	8 30	10 31	12 23	14 25	16 24	18 26	20 24	22 26	0 28	2 27	4 29	6 27
30	8 34		12 27	14 29	16 28	18 30	20 28	22 30	0 32	2 31	4 33	6 31
31	8 38		12 31		16 31		20 32	22 34		2 35		6 35

ASCENDANT TABLE FOR 32° N. LATITUDE

Key Number Total   Ascendant
(key number plus birth time)

18:00 - 19:22	Aries
19:23 - 20:58	Taurus
20:59 - 22:57	Gemini
22:58 - 1:14	Cancer
1:15 - 3:39	Leo
3:40 - 5:59	Virgo
6:00 - 8:21	Libra
8:22 - 10:42	Scorpio
10:43 - 13:02	Sagittarius
13:03 - 14:58	Capricorn
14:59 - 16:37	Aquarius
16:38 - 18:00	Pisces

Use this table to determine your Ascendant if you were born at or near 32°N latitude—that is, in or around such cities as Los Angeles, Atlanta, Albuquerque, New Orleans, Dallas, Houston, Phoenix, Charleston (S.C.), Miami, or anyplace else in the southern United States. Outside the United States, this would include North Africa, Israel, northern India, southern and central China, and southern Japan.

ASCENDANT TABLE FOR 42° N LATITUDE

Key Number Total   Ascendant
(key number plus birth time)

18:00 - 19:09	Aries
19:10 - 20:33	Taurus
20:34 - 22:27	Gemini
22:28 - 0:48	Cancer
0:49 - 3:23	Leo
3:24 - 5:59	Virgo
6:00 - 8:33	Libra
8:34 - 11:07	Scorpio
11:08 - 13:30	Sagittarius
13:31 - 15:23	Capricorn
15:24 - 16:50	Aquarius
16:51 - 17:59	Pisces

Use this table to determine your Ascendant if you were born at or near 42°N latitude—that is, in or around such cities as New York, Philadelphia, Boston, Washington, D.C., Cleveland, Chicago, Salt Lake City, Omaha, Denver, Portland, Detroit, or anyplace in the northern United States. Outside the United States, this would include Spain, Italy, Greece, southern Europe, southern Russia, northern China, Korea, and northern Japan.

ASCENDANT TABLE FOR 52° N LATITUDE

Key Number Total   **Ascendant**
(key number plus birth time)

Key Number Total	Ascendant
18:00 - 18:52	Aries
18:53 - 20:00	Taurus
20:01 - 21:45	Gemini
21:46 - 0:17	Cancer
0:18 - 3:06	Leo
3:07 - 5:59	Virgo
6:00 - 8:51	Libra
8:52 - 11:42	Scorpio
11:43 - 14:14	Sagittarius
14:15 - 16:00	Capricorn
16:01 - 17:08	Aquarius
17:09 - 17:59	Pisces

Use this table to determine your Ascendant if you were born at or near 52°N latitude, which includes Canada, Britain, northern Europe, and central and northern Russia.

ASCENDANT WORKSHEET

Your birth time (in 24-hour notation), **Standard time** . . . .

. . . .   ____:____

Birthday key number . . . .   ____:____

Total (if more than 24 hours.,
    subtract 24)   . . . .   ____:____

Look up your total in the right table for the latitude you were born at.

Your Ascendant   . . . .   _____

The Lunar or Monthly Cycle

It takes 27½ days for the moon to complete its cycle, and that cycle can be an important one in planning your work schedule—or your schedule for finding work. You can find out where the moon is on any given day by consulting most almanacs—*Old Moore's Almanac* even has a complete ephemeris of all the planets, which can be helpful in tracing other cycles as well. Avoid the popular *Old Farmer's Almanac*, because it gives moon positions in constellations (sixteen of them) rather than zodiacal signs. Many popular calendars give daily moon positions, including the St. Joseph's Aspirin calendar, which is given away free at drugstores around New Year's.

The most important time in the lunar cycle is when the moon is over your Ascendant. This will usually be the busiest time of the month for you, and you will tend to look better to others at this time. Therefore it is a good time for job interviews

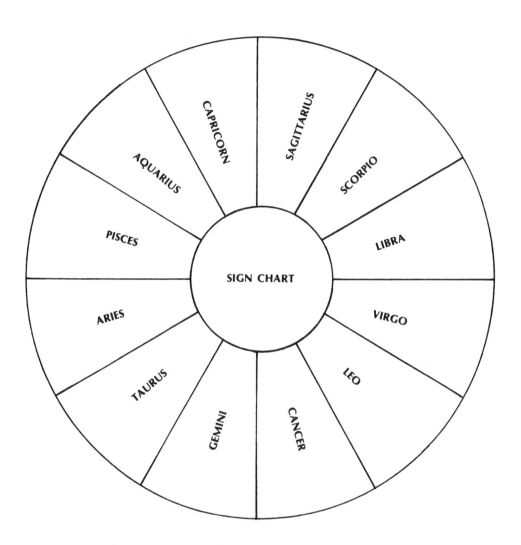

When counting signs, always count counterclockwise, beginning with the sign under consideration. Thus, Leo is the fifth sign from Aries, Libra is the seventh sign from Aries, and Capricorn is the tenth sign from Aries. A second example: Pisces is the seventh sign from Virgo, Sagittarius is the fourth sign from Virgo, and Taurus is the ninth sign from Virgo.

or for closing deals in your favor. Why this should be so is anybody's guess, but perhaps, as Dr. Lieber suggests, the moon has a pulling influence on everybody, and when it's in your Ascendant position, it pulls people in your direction.

Conversely, when the moon is in its opposite place, six signs away, you will generally find things a bit quieter and less likely to turn out in your favor.

The second time of importance in this cycle is when the moon is in the same sign as your sun. At this time you will likely feel a monthly energy peak. When the moon is opposite your sun (180° away—each sign equalling 30°, see Sign Chart), you'll feel an energy low and it's a more likely time to catch cold as well, because your resistance is lower.

If, as in about one out of twelve cases, your Ascendant falls in the seventh sign from your sun, the effects will tend to cancel out, and you'll just have to find out the lunar high points by observation over a period of time. In any case, it is well to watch the lunar rhythm, because it may trigger regular pockets of activity in certain other signs, depending on your natal planetary placements. When you establish a rhythm, it will give you the advantage of knowing what parts of the month are going to be busier in general so you won't overbook yourself at those time—rather, you should set them aside for important matters that need to be tended well.

There is a second, better documented lunar cycle (discussed briefly in Chapter 1), and that is the 29½-day phase cycle from full moon to full moon. You can find the phases of the moon listed not only in almanacs and calendars, but also in many newspapers. If the sky is clear, all you have to do is look up. If you don't see the moon day or night, it's the time of the new moon. If you see it at night, it's going from full to new; if you see it during the day, it's going from new to full, as a general rule of thumb. If it's the time of the full moon, the moon rises at sunset and you can't miss it.

As a categorical statement, it may be said that the full moon produces a higher state of tension and excitedness in human, animals, and plants. This is well documented by extensive research. Thus, at full moon judgment may be colored by these feelings—knowledge you can use to your advantage.

For instance, the full moon is a better time for partying or making love than for doing important work that requires a steady hand and clear judgment. Enjoyable pastimes where the unexpected is part of the fun use up that extra energy and tension in a positive, creative manner. To do more sober tasks at this time requires repression of those emotionally charged feelings. This attempt may prove difficult and will certainly adversely affect performance. It's a lousy time for a job interview, for example, because the general feeling of pressure both on you and on your potential employer, will not work in your favor. The same goes for important business deals, because all parties concerned will feel somewhat on edge and that will tend, at best, to make for doubts about the deal, and at worst, to make the whole thing blow up in your face. Be like the hardwood industrialists and cut your timber away from the full moon. The new moon also produces some tension, but not nearly so much, and it's much easier to use it creatively.

This is all good advice, based on firm statistics, but here's a personal example. For many years I have had the enjoyment of performing on summer evenings with a sea chanty group on the piers at New York City's South Street Seaport Museum. It's really a very pleasant pastime, singing the crusty old folk songs of working and drinking under the tall spars of the nineteenth-century square-riggers docked there.

But I have come to look with some trepidation upon those nights when the moon has reached its full. It's very dramatic, watching the fat orb of the moon rise over the East River and pulling the water up with it to its highest tide, just barely underneath the docks. But as a performer, you never know what to expect, either from the several hundred people in the audience or from the group itself. These nights are always our best or worst of the summer, depending on how we handle them. If we try to make ordered, well-designed sets of songs, everything inevitably falls apart and the evening is a bust. Guitar strings break, we forget the words, everything gets out of tune and sounds just awful. If, on the other hand, we just create our performance as we go along, everybody has a good time and the evening turns into a fun, spontaneous happening.

Our group doesn't make a living singing, so this is not really a crucial matter. But were we a struggling pop music group with an important audition or recording session on a full-moon night, it could be professional disaster and cause us to blow the one "big break" that everyone in the music biz is always looking for. Forewarned is forearmed.

The Solar or Yearly Cycle

Like the moon, the sun exerts a cyclic pull on us, but the pull is much stronger—it's what keeps the earth in orbit, determines the seasons, and keeps us all alive. The sun's cycle, 365¼ days, serves very much as an overall personal energy and health cycle and often determines what season of the year you will do best in.

One may look at the position of the sun at any time of year as a direction from which a positive, favorable, "sunny" pull is being exerted upon us all. When that pull is coming from the same direction as your Ascendant, then you get the benefit of that positive energy when people see you or deal with you. Thus that time of year will be busier for you and will often serve as the real starting point of your year in the professional sense. This can even be the case when you are in a profession where most of the work is done at a time of year when the sun is not near your Ascendant. I know a writer, for instance, with Leo on the Ascendant who gets most of his important commissions in the middle to late summer, when the sun is passing over his Ascendant, even though the publishing industry is considered dead at that time of year because everybody is on vacation. Somehow this writer manages to get what little work there is at that time, while others go hungry.

As a general rule, however, that kind of positioning is a real disadvantage. Sometimes there just isn't any work at your best time of year, so your best time is regularly wasted. It is better to choose a profession or industry where the major jobs and commissions are handed out at the time of year when the sun is passing over your Ascendant. This will put you automatically at the head of the line, all other factors being equal. When there is a break to be had, you'll be the first to get it.

When the sun is at the bottom of its Ascendant cycle, that is the seventh sign from the Ascendant, then you are likely to experience a quiet period in which less happens in general and fewer opportunities come your way. If you can take a vacation at this time, do so. You won't be missing much.

The other solar cycle worth considering centers around your birthday, a time when you are likely to have more energy than any other. This is a trend that will follow you to your grave, because it has been several times demonstrated statistically that

"There is a tide in the the affairs of men
Which, taken at the flood, leads on to fortune;
Omitted, all the voyage of their life
Is bound in shallows and in miseries."

—Julius Caesar, Act IV, Scene 3

significantly fewer people die in the months surrounding their birthdays than in the months further away from them. There have been various theories proposed to explain this, but nothing definitive. Whatever the reason, it would appear you have more real life force working for you around your birth date, and 6 months away from it you have less energy and are more susceptible to health problems. Therefore, perhaps the other most ideal time for a vacation would be 6 months after your birthday—an "unbirthday" celebration and recuperation. At the least, you should expect less to be happening at this time and count on fewer potential sources of extra income—and you should take extra care of your health. Get lots of vitamin C (I go on a grapefruit binge that time of year) and go easy on yourself so the local viruses won't pick you for their next victim.

Naturally, the relative positions of your Ascendant and your natal sun will determine a sort of double rhythm for the year, such that you will have a business activity peak followed by an energy peak or vice versa. They will occur together only if they both fall in the same sign. If they occur 6 months apart, you will be one of those unusual individuals who looks best when feeling worst, and vice versa. By keeping an eye on this combined cycle, you can try to plan things so it gives you the extra added push when you want it and you don't find yourself struggling through important matters at the very bottom of a cycle.

Another personal example: I have a Gemini Ascendant, so every year just as summer is about to begin (as the sun goes into Gemini), I get into gear. Unfortunately, the rest of the world is getting ready to take off for summer vacations, but I manage to

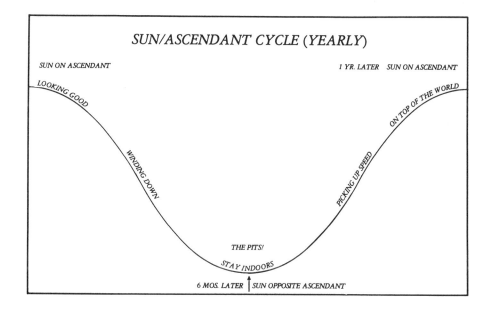

SUN/ASCENDANT CYCLE (YEARLY)

SUN ON ASCENDANT

1 YR. LATER   SUN ON ASCENDANT

LOOKING GOOD

ON TOP OF THE WORLD

WINDING DOWN

PICKING UP SPEED

THE PITS!

STAY INDOORS

6 MOS. LATER   SUN OPPOSITE ASCENDANT

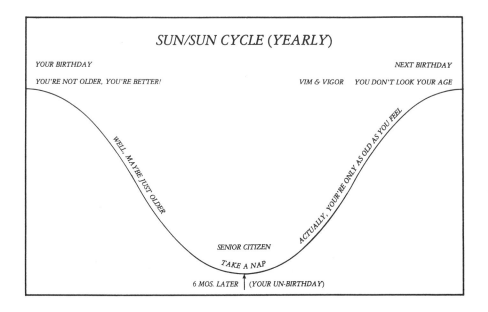

pick up whatever out-of-the-ordinary business is to be had at this time. This advantage is reinforced by the fact that my natal sun is in Leo, so I'm at an energy peak when everyone else is dropping from the heat in the dog days of August, or else off on a cool European vacation. But when the rest of the business world is busiest, during the fall, winter, and early spring, I'm neither looking nor feeling my best and it puts me at a real disadvantage. In effect, it tends to herd me into less-frequented areas in the pursuit of a living, so I have found myself writing about unusual topics and performing obscure music for most of my life. If I wanted to be in the mainstream, I'd be better off in the southern hemisphere where the seasons are reversed.

This is not to suggest that everyone with natal sun or Ascendant in summer signs should pack up and move to Australia, or is doomed to take second position in the everyday business world. It merely means that these people will have to struggle harder than their neighbors, all other things being equal, in order to reach the same spot, or be willing to go into areas that are more off the beaten track. Being naturally lazy, I chose the latter course, but whatever *your* choice, it helps to be aware of all the factors affecting it.

One final comment: Astrologers say that the sign of your Ascendant determines the nature of your physical appearance. Well, there's no proof of that as yet, but perhaps it's an explanation for the similarity of appearance of so many people within a given industry. I know I can spot a music biz type walking down the street by appearance alone—and the same goes for ad men, garment industry salesmen, and so on. Perhaps their Ascendants are just more naturally in tune with the yearly rhythm of their industries. It may be idle speculation, but it's thought-provoking.

SUN CYCLE TABLE

March 21 - April 21	the sun is traveling through **Aries**
April 22 - May 21	the sun is traveling through **Taurus**
May 22 - June 21	the sun is traveling through **Gemini**
June 22 - July 21	the sun is traveling through **Cancer**
July 22 - August 22	the sun is traveling through **Leo**
August 23 - September 22	the sun is traveling through **Virgo**
September 23 - October 23	the sun is traveling through **Libra**
October 24 - November 22	the sun is traveling through **Scorpio**
November 23 - December 21	the sun is traveling through **Sagittarius**
December 22 - January 21	the sun is traveling through **Capricorn**
January 22 - February 20	the sun is traveling through **Aquarius**
February 21 - March 20	the sun is traveling through **Pisces**

3

MARS:
THE 2-YEAR WORK-ENERGY CYCLE

In Gauquelin's studies, Mars was generally found to be strongly connected with athletes when rising or culminating, but whatever its position, it signifies the accumulation and expenditure of energy. Thus it is particularly associated with new jobs or new projects that take extra energy—more energy than would be required to continue an old job or project.

Mars' cycle is almost 2 years—about 1 year 11 months to be more exact. Its importance in career efforts does not appear to be its cycle in relation to the Ascendant, as with other planets, but its cycle relation to its natal position.

Every 2 years, when Mars returns to its natal place, there is an energy boost that often marks a change in job status or the taking on of a significant new project or commitment. Conversely, when Mars is in the seventh sign from its natal position, at the bottom of its cycle, the likelihood of a successful job change is at its lowest and current projects seem less stimulating. The desire for change and growth begins and comes to fruition at the next Mars return.

This is an important cycle to remember in job seeking, because chances of success are greatly enhanced when job hunting is done around the time Mars is returning to its natal place. When it is at its low point in the cycle, job seeking can still be successful, but the position desired may not be obtained, but rather a temporary job that can be changed when Mars gets back to its natal place. This happened recently to a client of mine who had been fired from her job (quite unfairly, I might add) and was out on the street looking for anything she could get. Unfortunately, she was just passing her Mars low and the prospects weren't good, at least not for the kind of job she wanted.

I advised her not to be picky and insist on exactly what she wanted, but rather to take something temporary and wait until her Mars return, when a job she really wanted would more likely come along. She did just that, taking a shop assistant position, though it was supposed to be a permanent job (never tell a prospective employer you intend to walk out as soon as something better comes along). About the time of her next Mars return, the office managing position she wanted, and was most qualified for,

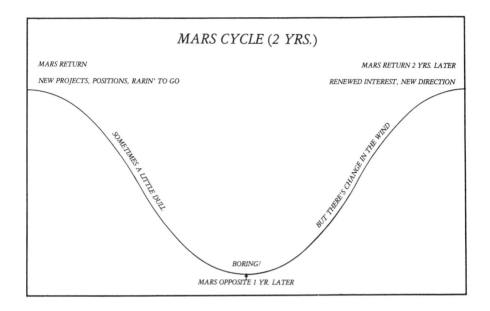

turned up and dropped right into her lap—this at a time when her apartment lease was up, so she could move thirty miles to where the job, and also the man she loved, was. A happy conclusion.

The Mars return does not always mean an actual job change—leaving one firm and going to another. It frequently means a change in job status—a new title, new responsibilities, high pay, within the same business or firm. So if you want a better chance of success when you ask for that raise you think you deserve, wait until Mars returns to its natal position before you approach your boss.

In the accompanying Mars table you can find both the position of your natal Mars and where Mars will be up through 2000. If you want more exact positions down to the degree, use an ephemeris such as the one in *Old Moore's Almanac* or in any standard astrological ephemeris. Pinpoint accuracy is not necessary, as events triggered by the Mars cycle tend to cluster within a month on either side of the Mars return, with no telling exactly when they'll happen. This is a period of raised energy and project activity where chances of moving up in the world are generally heightened.

It is a good idea in observing the Mars cycle, and all other cycles as well, to check out what it has done for you in the past so you have a better notion of exactly how it affects you personally. It can have a wide range of effects, depending on whether you work for a small or large company, own your own business, are a freelancer, or have switched professions. The table covers enough years so you can trace the cycles all the way back into your childhood, and establish a track record for the cycle in your life and gauge what changes it might bring in your future.

You may notice in the table that Mars sometimes stays in roughly the same place for as long as 8 months because of apparent retrogradation. In these instances there will be a lot of starts and stops of opportunity, with things not really resolving themselves until Mars starts moving along again as usual.

Remember, however, that like all cycles, this is just a general helpful influence. Your Mars return won't get you a new job or a raise unless you actively pursue one. Virtually all the major job changes I have had, for instance, have occurred on schedule around a Mars return, but I have also had Mars returns where nothing new happened at all because I was not in pursuit of anything or was working on a long-range project that could not be completed at that time. To quote a tired old astrologers' saying: The stars impel, they don't compel. In the end it's up to you, but you can use planetary cycles to help you out along the way.

MARS TABLE
Positions for 15th of the Month

	Jan.	Feb.	Mar.	Apr.	May	June	July	Aug.	Sep.	Oct.	Nov.	Dec.
1920	LI	SC	SC	SC	LI	LI	SC	SC	SA	SA	CP	AQ
1921	PI	AR	AR	TA	GE	GE	CA	LE	LE	VI	LI	LI
1922	SC	SC	SA	SA	SA	SA	SA	SA	CP	CP	AQ	AQ
1923	PI	AR	TA	TA	GE	CA	CA	LE	VI	VI	LI	SC
1924	SC	SA	CP	CP	AQ	AQ	PI	PI	AQ	AQ	PI	PI
1925	AR	TA	TA	AQ	CA	CA	LE	VI	VI	LI	SC	SC
1926	SA	CP	CP	AQ	PI	AR	AR	TA	TA	TA	TA	TA
1927	TA	TA	GE	GE	CA	LE	LE	VI	LI	LI	SC	SA
1928	SA	SA	AQ	PI	PI	AR	TA	GE	GE	CA	CA	CA
1929	GE	GE	CA	CA	LE	LE	VI	VI	LI	SC	SC	SA
1930	CP	AQ	AQ	PI	AR	TA	GE	GE	CA	CA	LE	LE
1931	LE	LE	CA	LE	LE	VI	VI	LI	LI	SC	SA	CP
1932	CP	AQ	PI	AR	TA	TA	GE	CA	CA	LE	VI	VI
1933	VI	VI	VI	VI	VI	VI	LI	LI	SC	SA	SA	CP
1934	AQ	PI	AR	AR	TA	GE	GE	CA	LE	LE	VI	LI
1935	LI	LI	LI	LI	LI	LI	LI	SC	SC	SA	CP	AQ
1936	PI	PI	AR	TA	GE	GE	CA	LE	LE	VI	LI	LI
1937	SC	SC	SA	SA	SC	SC	SC	SA	SA	CP	AQ	AQ
1938	PI	AR	TA	TA	GE	CA	CA	LE	VI	VI	LI	SC

Year												
1939	SC	SA	SA	CP	CP	AQ	AQ	CP	CP	AQ	AQ	PI
1940	AR	AR	TA	GE	GE	CA	LE	LE	VI	VI	LI	SC
1941	SA	SA	CP	AQ	AQ	PI	AR	AR	AR	AR	AR	AR
1942	TA	TA	GE	GE	CA	LE	LE	VI	VI	LI	SC	SC
1943	SA	CP	AQ	AQ	PI	AR	TA	TA	GE	GE	GE	GE
1944	GE	GE	GE	CA	CA	LE	VI	VI	LI	SC	SC	SA
1945	CP	AQ	AQ	PI	AR	TA	TA	GE	CA	CA	LE	LE
1946	CA	CA	CA	CA	LE	LE	VI	LI	LI	SC	SA	SA
1947	CP	AQ	PI	AR	AR	TA	GE	CA	CA	LE	LE	VI
1948	VI	LE	LE	LE	LE	VI	VI	LI	SC	SC	SA	CP
1949	AQ	PI	PI	AR	TA	GE	GE	CA	LE	LE	VI	VI
1950	LI	LI	LI	VI	VI	LI	LI	SC	SC	SA	CP	CP
1951	AQ	PI	AR	TA	TA	GE	CA	CA	LE	VI	VI	LI
1952	LI	SC	SC	SC	SC	SC	SC	SC	SA	CP	CP	AQ
1953	AR	AR	AR	TA	GE	GE	CA	LE	VI	VI	LI	LI
1954	SC	SA	SA	CP	CP	CA	SA	SA	CP	CP	AQ	PI
1955	PI	AR	TA	GE	GE	PI	LE	LE	VI	LI	LI	SC
1956	SA	SA	CP	AQ	AQ	PI	PI	PI	PI	PI	PI	AR
1957	AR	TA	TA	GE	GE	CA	LE	VI	VI	LI	SC	SC
1958	SA	CP	CP	AQ	PI	AR	AR	TA	TA	GE	TA	TA
1959	TA	GE	GE	CA	CA	LE	LE	VI	LI	LI	SC	SA

Year												
1960	CP	CP	AQ	PI	AR	AR	TA	GE	GE	CA	CA	CA
1961	CA	CA	CA	CA	LE	LE	VI	VI	LI	SC	SA	SA
1962	CP	AQ	PI	PI	AR	TA	GE	GE	CA	LE	LE	LE
1963	LE	LE	LE	LE	VI	VI	VI	SC	SC	SC	SA	CP
1964	AQ	AQ	PI	AR	TA	TA	GE	CA	LE	LE	VI	VI
1965	VI	VI	VI	VI	VI	VI	LI	LI	SC	SA	CP	CP
1966	AQ	PI	AQ	AR	AR	TA	CA	LE	CA	VI	VI	LI
1967	LI	SC	SC	LI	LI	LI	LI	SC	SA	SA	CP	AQ
1968	PI	PI	AR	TA	GE	GE	CA	LE	LE	VI	LI	LI
1969	SC	SC	SA	TA	TA	SA	SA	SA	SA	CP	LI	PI
1970	PI	AR	SC	TA	TA	CA	LE	LE	VI	VI	SC	SC
1971	SC	SA	CP	CP	AQ	AQ	AQ	AQ	AQ	AQ	PI	PI
1972	AR	TA	TA	GE	CA	CA	LE	LE	VI	LI	SC	SC
1973	SA	CP	CP	AQ	PI	PI	AR	TA	TA	TA	AR	AR
1974	TA	TA	GE	GE	CA	LE	LE	VI	LI	LI	SC	SA
1975	SA	CP	AQ	PI	AR	AR	TA	GE	GE	GE	CA	GE
1976	GE	GE	GE	GE	LE	LE	VI	VI	LI	SC	SC	SA
1977	CP	AQ	AQ	CA	TA	TA	TA	LI	CA	CA	LE	LE
1978	LE	CA	CA	PI	AR	VI	VI	CA	LI	SC	SA	CP
1979	CP	AQ	AQ	AR	AR	VI	GE	CA	CA	LE	LE	VI
1980	VI	VI	VI	LE	VI	VI	LI	LI	SC	SA	SA	CP

Year												
1981	AQ	PI	PI	AR	TA	GE	GE	CA	LE	LE	VI	VI
1982	LI	LI	LI	LI	LI	LI	SC	SC	SA	CP	CP	AQ
1983	AQ	PI	AR	TA	TA	GE	CA	LE	LE	VI	VI	LI
1984	SC	SC	SC	SC	SC	SC	SC	SC	SA	CP	CP	AQ
1985	PI	AR	AR	TA	GE	CA	CA	LE	VI	VI	LI	SC
1986	SC	SA	SA	SA	CP	CP	CP	CP	CP	AQ	AQ	PI
1987	AR	AR	TA	GE	GE	CA	LE	LE	VI	LI	LI	SC
1988	SA	CP	CP	AQ	AQ	PI	AR	AR	AR	AR	AR	AR
1989	AR	TA	GE	GE	CA	LE	LE	VI	VI	LI	SC	SA
1990	SA	CP	AQ	AQ	PI	AR	TA	TA	GE	GE	GE	TA
1991	TA	GE	GE	GE	LE	LE	VI	VI	LI	SC	SC	SA
1992	CP	CP	AQ	PI	AR	TA	TA	GE	CA	CA	CA	CA
1993	CA	CA	CA	CA	LE	LE	VI	LI	LI	SC	SA	SA
1994	CP	AQ	PI	AR	AR	TA	GE	CA	CA	LE	LE	VI
1995	VI	LE	LE	LE	LE	VI	VI	SC	SC	SC	SA	CP
1996	AQ	PI	PI	AR	TA	GE	GE	SC	LE	LE	VI	VI
1997	LI	LI	VI	VI	VI	LI	LI	LE	SC	SA	CP	AQ
1998	AQ	PI	AR	TA	TA	GE	CA	CA	LE	VI	VI	LI
1999	LI	SC	SC	SC	LI	LI	SC	SC	SA	CP	CP	AQ
2000	PI	AR	TA	TA	GE	CA	CA	LE	LE	VI	LI	LI

AR— Aries
TA— Taurus
GE— Gemini
CA— Cancer

LE— Leo
VI— Virgo
LI— Libra
SC— Scorpio

SA— Sagittarius
CP— Capricorn
AQ— Aquarius
PI— Pisces

4

JUPITER:
YOUR PRODUCTIVITY
AND OPPORTUNITY CYCLE

Jupiter is the planet of opportunity and productivity, and its cycle of 12 years is the key to your overall career and personal success. Its help cannot be overestimated, but proper timing in its use is essential if its effects are to be lasting.

Jupiter's maximum benefits accrue when it is in your Ascendant sign (see appropriate Ascendant Table in Chapter 2) and the sign immediately following it. During these times your personal influence and money-making potential will be at their peak. You will be riding high, in terms of both personal image and outward success, and the foundations you lay in those areas will have to support you for another 12 years, so lay them well and avoid the very real temptation to glory and frolic in what may be only temporary good times. Very many persons waste much of the fruitful energies given abundantly at this time, when every opportunity and contact made should be industriously recorded and followed up. It is not always easy to do this because of the natural ego elation that accompanies unasked for or unexpected good fortune. Too often people take personal credit for improvement rather than recognize it as a temporary cycle period.

Jupiter Cycle No. 1

Since Jupiter represents to the world at large the new, the profitable, and the exciting, the sign through which it is passing may be considered a filter through which the world sees these concepts. When it is passing through your Ascendant sign, therefore, your personal appearance takes on these qualities in the eyes of others. For a time your appear newer, more profitable, and exciting, not neccessarily through any virtue of your own. If you are aware of this, you can take advantage of it to infuse yourself with those qualities and make a special effort to present yourself in that light. This will establish you as an achiever and innovator in your field, something you can then draw upon during later and less bountiful cycles.

When Jupiter is in your Ascendant sign, your personal effect on people will be maximized and you will find yourself more confident. It is a time to make your mark in a very up-front manner, by presenting yourself in person to those who may benefit you rather than relying on agents or even the mails to do the job for you. It is your own physical presence that has the effect, and you should use it to the maximum. Your best position is out in front of the public, even if that is not normally the most comfortable spot for you. At this point, it is where your greatest advantage lies.

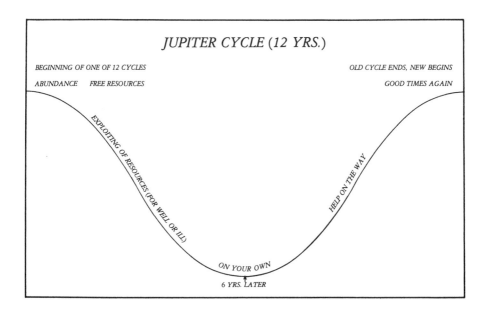

It is most important not to bask in the extra attention you may receive at this time. You won't receive this kind of attention for another 12 years, so take note of every favorable reaction you get and chase it down. Try to develop a lasting relationship, or at least the beginnings of one, with the people and companies you contact at this time. They may bail you out of many a difficulty later. Incidentally, the advantage applies to intimate relationships as well, and lovers you take at this time will come back again and again because they will have an image of you as youthful and dynamic. The only disadvantage you have to watch out for is excessive weight gain, something that is also associated with this cycle. You can avoid this if you work off the additional energies in diligent exploitation of the advantages and opportunities presented at this time.

Once this year-long phase has ended, it is time to start abandoning strategies based on the primary power of personal appearance and developing new ones that are more oriented to your potential as a money handler. Solidify the contacts and advantages you gained in the first cycle, and begin to shift to the next. Do it carefully, as what you have achieved must suffice in those areas for the next 12 years, while the focus of creativity and development shifts to other areas.

That's show biz . . . Jupiter cycle No. 1

Jupiter Cycle No. 2

In the year Jupiter is in the sign following that of your Ascendant, most of your creative focus will be on finance and personal possessions. At this time you will develop habits and precedents that will largely influence your handling of money and others' trust in you to do so for the next 12 years.

Most people find that more money is generally available to them at this time, though this may only be a larger cash flow rather than greater overall financial security. But this time usually brings greater financial opportunity, and is therefore exceedingly important to your career.

The second cycle is usually a critical time for laying the foundations for your enterprises for the next 12 years, at least in a financial sense. Good judgment and care at this time can provide you with ample support for future development, while injudicious use of funds or aimless and confused spending may mean that you will spend more than a decade floundering about without sufficient support for what may be excellent and deserving talents and goals. This is unfortunate, but it reflects the value society places on material things and their management.

Large amounts of money may be spent at this time—or at least more than your normal cash flow. This holds true if you find yourself in charge of others' money. In either case you will be given more responsibility than usual in this area, often because you are given more credit for your ability to handle money than you deserve. Therefore, it is to your benefit to learn how to live up to the fiscal responsibility rather than simply revel in the extra resources. This is true even if the extra resources available are only minimally greater than usual, or simply greater than those of the people around you.

You will find in this period that you have to bring to earth the opportunities you gained in the previous year. Now you have to prove that the confidence you inspired a year ago will be borne out in reality. The glory has worn off and you have to prove your substance. If you carefully cultivated the previous opportunities, then with reasonable diligence you should reap fairly substantial profits. If you ignored them, then you have little to gain in this period except basic experience in handling funds and resources. This experience in itself is no mean opportunity, for it will serve you well in the period of intellectual creativity and stimulation that comes next.

It is especially important to force yourself to become involved with the details of money management at this time, even if you are pursuing a career (for example, in the arts or sciences) where such goals may be secondary to more abstract or idealistic preoccupations. Economic demands suffuse every facet of our lives, no matter what our profession, and ignoring an opportunity to understand and control them will only put you at a disadvantage for the rest of the 12-year cycle.

To illustrate how a person ignorant of these critical cycles can unknowingly waste them, let us take the example of a certain musician with Gemini Ascendant. When Jupiter entered Gemini in 1965, he was given tremendous exposure by a conglomerate with a major record label. His personal image was just right for the youth-oriented music of the time. He was given personal introductions to and support by many of the most influential people in the music business.

But, being young at the time and not truly knowing the nature of what was happening to him, he let the sudden fame and exposure go to his head. He spent his time pursuing the groupies, drugs, and ample personal admiration that was to be had at the time.

The result: When Jupiter had passed on and the company was looking for new talent, he was out. He hadn't taken advantage of the opportunities presented and they had slipped through his fingers.

Then he got a second chance, but he blew that one, too. As Jupiter moved into Cancer, he took a large sum of money that he had and made investments in the music business. Everything seemed very positive (as it always does with Jupiter), so instead of giving full attention to the detailed use of his money, he turned to other pursuits, leaving money management in the hands of others. Once Jupiter passed the money was gone, and the unfortunate musician found himself left behind. Eventually he was forced to start anew in a different career. If he had known the true nature of the events that were happening to him, he might well have saved himself years of struggle and failure.

Jupiter Cycle No. 3

The year when Jupiter is in the third sign from the Ascendant is not as critical a period financially as the first two, at least not in an immediate sense. The immediate pressure to produce tangible financial results slackens, but the third cycle is an extremely important period in the long run because it is a cycle of ideas.

This tends to be a time when inventiveness and technical creativity flow particularly well, You may find that you come up with a great many more ideas, bright and otherwise, than you can possibly use at the moment. For every brainstorm that has immediate practical use, there will be ten that don't have much relevance to your current situation, which you will be tempted to discard.

Don't.

Instead, file your ideas *on paper* (not in the back of your mind, where they'll get lost) for use at another time. They may lie in your files for years, but the chances are you'll be happy you've got them miles down the road when you're not feeling so inventive. This period is one of heightened intellectual capacity that won't recur for 12 years, so throwing away ideas that sprout now is like tossing out surplus wheat during a time of plenty—when famine comes, you'll be out of luck.

A small example of this is an inventor I know who dreamed up some plans for making electric jewelry back in the sixties during his third Jupiter cycle. It was a nice idea, but not really practicable, since the subminiaturized circuitry necessary to it hadn't been developed yet, nor had batteries that could sustain it. So, after considerable research and design effort, he chucked the whole thing and pursued other ideas that had more immediate potential.

Six years later he was approached by someone in a major jewelry firm who, remembering his earlier efforts, asked him to help design some prototypes, now that the technology had advanced enough to make the idea practical. Unfortunately, our foolish inventor had lost all his previous work and turned out to be of little use to the company. Thus he forfeited what could have been an interesting and lucrative opportunity.

Fortunately, he wasn't entirely out of luck since during that same Jupiter period he had designed some electronic instruments that were not technically feasible but whose plans he had retained anyway. Not long after the jewelry fiasco he had the opportunity to implement those plans and got profitably involved with patenting and producing prototypes for the inventions he fortunately had not thrown away.

So, however harebrained the schemes you turn up during the third Jupiter cycle, don't toss them out just because they don't have immediate use. Stow them away in a safe place and they'll reward you years later.

Conversely, ideas born at this time that others think useful may, in fact, be of much less value than they seem. People will tend to view you as a fountainhead of originality during this period and may place greater value on your schemes than they deserve. Here it is very important to be your own severest critic so that you don't get involved in losing projects for which you will have to bear the blame later, just because somebody thought you had a brilliant idea at the time.

As in all cycles, timing is important here. You should make a special effort to tie up loose ends as the third cycle draws to a close because your ingenuity will begin to diminish and your previous efforts will have to stand by themselves as your direction changes toward more important inner considerations. Make sure you have recorded *all* your inspirations. Then you may move on in confidence that you have used the period to its utmost and that it will profit you at various times in the coming 12 years.

Jupiter Cycle No. 4

As Jupiter moves into your fourth sign from your Ascendant, you will find that your attention and inspiration move toward inner personal concerns and home matters. Many people either relocate this year or spend a lot of time renovating and expanding the home they have. This is the cycle in which you structure the way you're going to live for the coming 12 years. This is the time when you establish the type of home life you will draw upon or strive to maintain for that period of time.

If you neglect this area during this cycle, you will probably continue to neglect it for 12 years to come. That means your living quarters will be either unimportant to you for the next 12 years, or simply a pain in the neck. If you are in a profession where a strong social image is required for success, neglecting this opportunity can be a real disaster, but if you work in an area where professional efforts are unrelated to home life, it just means that you'll be missing something that might provide you with extra enjoyment and serve as a respite from the difficulties of your job.

This is also true of the spiritual realm, as the fourth Jupiter cycle is one of the inner home and refuge—a person's spiritual foundation and family. It is an excellent time to reestablish or strengthen personal and family ties that may have been neglected in the previous few years when your outlook was much more exteriorized because of the nature of events around you. Events in the outside world will calm down a bit, or at least hold their course, and this will give you the opportunity to strengthen and fortify

Moving day   Jupiter cycle No. 4

the foundation of your character and concentrate on your inner self.

Spiritual advice may seem out of place in a career book, but truly successful careers depend upon integration of the inner and outer personality so the individual can function as a whole person in the decision-making processes that determine career success or failure. An unbalanced person will always be at a disadvantage, and even when successful will not be living up to his or her full potential.

If the personality is focused in this direction during the fourth Jupiter cycle, an integration and balance will be achieved that will be a resource of strength for the coming 12 years so that failure may be endured and success be more fully achieved. A strong inner foundation will also have a particularly beneficial effect on your efforts in the next Jupiter cycle, the fifth, which is one of pleasure and creativity. It will make that period far more productive and rewarding. It is hard to come up with cut-and-dried examples of the use or misuse of this cycle being the direct cause of career success or failure, but I have seen many examples of the well-used period creating greater personal and family harmony. That, certainly, can only help and strengthen career efforts, as well as being a worthy goal in itself.

Jupiter Cycle No. 5

When Jupiter reaches the fifth sign from the Ascendant, it brings a particularly enjoyable period of spontaneous creativity that is invaluable to anyone involved in work where creativity is required. For writers, artists, and musicians, it is a time when the muse never deserts you and you wake up at night with new inspirations and rush to set them down before they escape you. It has a certain similarity to the third cycle, because of the spontaneous occurrence of new ideas, but here they are of a more inspirational and less utilitarian nature.

Even in career areas that are not basically aesthetically oriented—say, accounting —this is a period in which you can make work methods and design accord better with your own human needs and those of your colleagues. It is a time of making anything you do more fun, and any methods you can devise to do this will make the next 12 years a lot more pleasant to live through, and probably more profitable as well.

In general, it is a period to learn to play at what you do, and to turn work into play. This is particularly valuable if you are in a position to restructure others' work habits as well as your own. For instance, one office manager I knew used the period to rearrange the schedules of her whole staff in such a way that they enjoyed more freedom, got more work done, and made more money in the process. And it was all because she had found a method to make the job more challenging and yet more creative at the same time.

The danger here is that the opportunities to enjoy yourself may simply be too many and too tempting at this time, so you may find yourself neglecting necessary tasks in favor of more pleasurable, if less profitable, activities. It is hard to say what direction to take here; you will have to weigh the value of your present enjoyment against the pleasure a full bank account will give you in the future. Frequently this is a time in which personal involvements such as love affairs, vacation opportunities, and other pleasurable possibilities enticingly interpose themselves between you and your work schedule. Only you can be the judge of what to pursue, but some kind of balance is probably preferable.

This period brings not only love involvements, but frequently their result: children. It's amazing how many people wind up becoming parents at this time, either by accident or because it seemed like such a nice idea at the time. Children need care for a lot longer than a 12-year cycle, and can be devastating to a career, so use your head and avoid following spur-of-the-moment feelings. As heartless as it may sound, children are a distinct disadvantage to almost any career, unless you're a professional parent, and from a career standpoint are to be avoided, at least until you are in a position where they will be a minimal burden and you will be able to support them properly and spend enough time with them. That's a tall order, and one that far too few parents have proved able to fill.

Jupiter Cycle No. 6

As Jupiter moves into the sixth sign from your Ascendant, you will likely find yourself bothered by, perhaps obsessed with, the details of your work. At this time you may be stuck doing comparatively menial tasks, and you are not likely to feel your career is rushing on apace. This may be the case even if you are relatively successful at what you are doing. I remember spending seemingly endless hours stuffing envelopes and preparing mailers during this period, even though I was the president of the corporation that was doing the mailing!

Dull as this period may be, it is important to pay attention to everything that comes up, even if it seems unbearably dreary. It is said that a good boss is one who knows how to do every task there is in the company, and this is the time that tests your abilities in this area. The first time this cycle peak occurs in your professional life, you may be stuck in some lowly job, doing something that bores you to death. By the time the cycle recurs, you may be halfway (or all the way) to the top, but find you have to take the time to relearn old jobs and become acquainted with new ones that have developed since you moved on to greater things.

Neglecting this necessity can be fatal to your career and harmful to the company you work for, particularly if it's your own. A business is only as strong as its ability to put out a product—and that includes every one of the details that such output requires. I know one person in publishing who started his own company on a shoestring, doing everything himself, and before long had a successful operation with a number of employees. He just assumed that increasing sales meant more money, so he left it up to his employees to keep cranking out the books while he moved on to bigger and better ideas.

What he didn't realize is that at a certain level the mechanisms for handling the flood of details involved in significantly larger sales become much more expensive in relation to the increased income. At this level computerized inventory and other new lower- and middle-management methods must be adopted in order to make the transition from a small to a middle-sized company. My friend, however, had his mind on other things, and it wasn't until the company began to lose money and he had to lay off a number of employees and do their work himself that he faced the situation and came up with the necessary solutions. If he had kept his eye on the details, he would never have gone through the experience of nearly losing his company and having to drag it back up by the bootstraps.

This is the sort of thing you have to keep your eye on all the time, of course, but in the sixth Jupiter cycle attention to details is particularly important, indeed crucial. If you take the time and patience now, life will be a lot easier in the next 12 years.

Snowed under   Jupiter cycle No. 6

Jupiter Cycle No. 7

When Jupiter has moved to the seventh sign from your Ascendant, it is 180° away from the original position we began with. Since a cycle is a recurring circle, we may say that this is really the bottom point of Jupiter cycle No. 1. Whereas No. 1 is concerned with the projection of your personality toward others, this cycle is concerned with the projection of others' personalities toward you. It is a time when partners and partnership in general will be of particular significance and help to you, and it is an ideal time to receive help through the efforts of others.

Thus the seventh cycle is a good time to get others to front for you, to let them do the selling while you stay behind the scenes. It is a time to soft-sell yourself and encourage others to come forward and do their thing. Very often you will have the opportunity to form close working partnerships, and you should be ready for as much give and take as possible, even though that means submerging your ego more than you would like. Treat this as a time when *others* are in the ascendancy and take full advantage of what they have to offer. To be very self-assertive now will be seen by

Your partner steals the show   Jupiter cycle No. 7

others as quite inappropriate and will be detrimental to your interests. This is partly because you are at the low end of cycle No. 1, so ego assertion is poor, and partly because it is unwise to reject the help of others when it is readily available.

This is also the peak of the 12-year cycle of learning to use others to your advantage. The opportunities presented by this period, if properly handled, will enable you to gain the skills and techniques of using outside aids in your endeavors. Ignore these opportunities and you will find yourself having to go it alone when the going gets rough.

This time may prove difficult, particularly for the independent-minded, because sometimes you will have to rely entirely on your partner or partners for income or moral support. That is not always good for your self-esteem, but swallow your pride and be thankful for the help you are getting. Things will change soon enough, so learn your lesson while you can: "No man is an island," and all that.

As well as being a time for taking advantage of the benefits of partnership, the seventh cycle is a good time to seek out and get to know the strengths and weaknesses of your adversaries. Study your competition and seek out their flaws, making sure that you correct those same defects in yourself. Then in the future you will be far better prepared to do battle with your competitors, even when, as so often happens in the business world, they turn out to be your former partners. The better you understood them when they were helping you, the less threat they'll be when they are opposing you.

Jupiter Cycle No. 8

As Jupiter proceeds into the eighth sign from your Ascendant, the focus will shift from establishing partnerships and equal work contracts to money management and learning to get the most out of a comparatively meager cash supply. This is the opposite of the No. 2 cycle, in which cash flow was high. Now, not only will your available cash be low, but more than likely you will have to handle others' funds.

This is a time when you will have to make every penny count, however well you may be doing, and it is not generally a good time for fiscal innovation. It is usually a good time to review and streamline traditional methods and come to a better and more active understanding of what makes them work. In a sense, it is similar to the experience of cycle No. 6, where great attention to details is required, except that here the emphasis is on attending to cash flow. You will have to establish your credibility as a responsible money handler, which is essential in a business world built on credit and previously established track records in money management.

Thus you must pick up every fiscal stitch so that the accountings you make either to superiors or to the bank (or, God forbid, the IRS!) are beyond reproach. You must particularly avoid incurring unnecessary debt, even to the extent of cutting back operations to avoid it. A friend of mine, a freelance writer, made the mistake of living off his revolving Master Charge account like there was no tomorrow during this period, and worse, failed to make his payments on time. The result was he lost his credit rating, and despite the fact that he made good on the entire loan, he was unable to get it back. Since he doesn't have a regular job, it may be years before he reestablishes a normal credit rating—and all because of a few late payments at the wrong time! It doesn't sound very fair, but that's the way the system works. It was particularly ironic in my friend's case, as he had his highest credit rating while working for less than he makes now for a company that went bankrupt because it couldn't pay its bills!

For those normally inclined to conservative fiscal policy, personal and corporate, this will not be a difficult period—in fact, they will do quite well and gain from their financial philosophy. But for those of a more speculative nature, this period can be a disaster unless they rein in their impulses and reserve them for appropriate times.

This, in a nutshell, is the advantage you get from being aware of cycles in general. There is a right and a wrong time for almost every different kind of policy during your career, and it is the timing that makes for success or failure, not the basic policies themselves. There is a time for every purpose under heaven, as the Old Testament says, and the trick is knowing which times are suited for which purposes. That is what career cycle study is all about.

Jupiter Cycle No. 9

When Jupiter gets into the ninth sign from your Ascendant, it will very often mark a critical concept-changing time that will alter your entire approach to your career. Whereas cycle No. 3 increased the ability of invention and specific problem solving, this cycle increases your ability to see the overall picture and come up with new directions for your career or for the field in which you are involved.

This often marks a time of profound reconsideration of the direction you have been taking and can be the beginning of a turn-around that will take you into a whole new life pattern or career. Despite the changes that may occur here, do not expect too much immediate effect or gain, as it will take the rest of the 12-year cycle (till Jupiter is again here) to realize the dreams and concepts you cook up here. But it probably will be the touchstone of the coming years as far as intellectual direction and development are concerned.

It is important in viewing the new ideas and concepts that may surface at this point not to simply abandon everything that went before in order to follow what may seem to be the only appropriate path. It takes a long time to become proficient and successful at a new career, or even to solidify and make practicable major changes in the one you're already in. Rather, a gradual approach is desired so that you will not (a) starve to death trying to compete in a new area in which you don't yet have proficiency or (b) make a fool of yourself trying to push through not-yet-matured ideas in your current field and have them rejected despite their merit. It is one thing to postulate a change, another thing entirely to make it work and make a living from it.

For example, what you are reading right now is the result of concepts that came about in my last ninth cycle, concepts of taking old-time astrology out of its superstitious mold of prognostication and combining it with established and workable cycles in human experience in order to make it understandable, accessible, and practical. That was only a beginning. I had to pursue a long road, throwing out a good half of traditional astrological lore as pure nonsense and integrating the other half with more legitimate cycle study,

New horizons   Jupiter cycle No. 9

human growth psychology, and plain common sense. As of this writing, I am able to look at it as an accomplished fact and move on to new directions in my current ninth Jupiter cycle peak.

Essentially, what you do in this cycle is get an important concept (or concepts) and then spend 12 years filling in the details. It is an exercise in holding to and refining an initial idea or direction so that it turns into a significant and well-wrought career or an important addition to the knowledge of your profession. But the chances are this idea is what you will make your reputation on, so it's worth every bit of the effort.

Jupiter Cycle No. 10

As Jupiter enters the tenth sign from your Ascendant, you will find yourself making a career commitment based on the concepts of the last cycle. This may mean shifting the emphasis of the area you are currently in or taking up a new career altogether.

In general, this will be a time of increase in your reputation, though the size of your bank account may not reflect it. In most businesses money comes from delivering the goods, not from a good reputation. Indeed, this period may present some difficulty if your reputation begins to promise more than you're really worth, because if you disappoint others now, it can have a bad effect on future dealings for some time to come.

A stock market analyst I know got a not entirely deserved reputation during this cycle for infallibly predicting which way the market would go on a day-to-day basis. He was good, but not that good. As a result, several people invested more money than they could really afford on his advice and unfortunately took a hard fall when his advice proved faulty. His reputation quickly turned to mud and he has a hard time finding investors now, even though his own investments are doing well. He should have been more cautious and not allowed his investors to take such a risk (even though it was their idea) solely on their inflated confidence in him.

On the other hand, the self-confidence this period can bring can be very helpful in successfully launching a career, even though its financial rewards may not be immediate. All efforts will be turned to your goals, and temporary setbacks will be more easily overcome because of a basic belief in your direction and an enthusiasm for your work. In general, you will get a good outside response to your efforts and at least nominal, if not heavily financial, support from others around you.

If there is a particular lesson to be learned here, it is how to create for yourself a good public image that you can live up to and be happy with. A craftily written résumé can do wonders for you at this time—just make sure you can really perform all the prodigies it claims for you. Since the period is essentially favorable anyway, it's better to keep your résumé short and to the point, with perhaps a hint of a suggestion that a lot of interesting stuff has been left out.

This is, of course, the bottom or opposite of the No. 4 cycle, so you may have little time for home life, but if you used your last No. 4 cycle judiciously, that should not interfere with your efforts. Rather, you should be able to spend full time carving out the kind of reputation and career you have your sights set on, so that when future advantages present themselves—as they will in the next cycle—you will have such a good grip on things that you will be able to use the advantages fully.

On your way   Jupiter cycle No. 10

Jupiter Cycle No. 11

As Jupiter moves into the eleventh sign from your Ascendant, opportunity will knock, particularly in the guise of helpful (and, hopefully, well-heeled) connections. If your goals are well defined and your past accomplishments well documented, you can use these pieces of fortune to greatest benefit. Here you are in a period when other people will be looking at you in a creative light, wanting to make use of your talents for their profit and yours. If you have a good grip on things, you'll be able to steer these people in the direction you desire, thus maximizing the benefits that will accrue to you. If you're just drifting, they'll either find you of little use or they'll use you entirely to their own ends, thus minimizing your profit from the deal.

At this time you should not hesitate to set your sights high and go for the very best, in both the people you meet and the projects you pursue. You will find more favor in high places, such as your company superiors or major movers in your field, than among your colleagues and contemporaries, so don't spend too much time in idle fraternizing. The time is better spent alone working on your projects or currying the acquaintance of those who would significantly help your career.

As a result, this can be the time when the money and opportunity to forward your career finally crystallize. Since you are in the downside of the No. 5 cycle, you will probably not feel as spontaneous and creative as you might like, but this is a time that is better earmarked for actualization of previously created ideas and directions. You may find that the creativity comes more from your benefactors, who are finding new and profitable uses for your talents.

If there is one thing you should not do in this period, it's look a gift horse in the mouth. True, you may be risking exploitation if you do not carefully examine offers you receive or get a lawyer to ponder the clauses in a contract, but this period will quickly pass, and with it will go the opportunities as well if you have not jumped at them. Remember, particularly early in your career, the chances are you need the opportunities, and the people offering them, a lot more than they need you. If you are balky or suspicious (particularly if something seems too good to believe), you may find yourself high and dry on the shore while someone else is riding your boat out to sea. Act as if you are fully worthy of the company you are trying to keep (even if you feel a little out of your depth) and you'll be a lot more likely to keep it. You can become a hard bargainer later when you're secure enough to have a position to bargain from. That position is a year or two in the future, so take what's offered and make the best of a good thing.

Jupiter Cycle No. 12

Whether you have fully utilized the previous cycle or not, when Jupiter goes into the twelfth sign from your Ascendant you will enter a period of preparation out of which you will launch yourself into the world with a bang when the overall Jupiter/Ascendant cycle begins anew. Usually this is a period of much work and production behind the scenes, bringing to fruition the projects or products you started on in the previous cycle.

Often this cycle requires considerable effort, but if you are organized and have established a direction, you will experience a feeling of imminent success that will give you the necessary energy to complete your tasks well. If you haven't got a real direction, this may seem like a period of floundering, of looking for success and not finding it, of waiting for lightning to strike and start your career moving again.

In either case, this may also be a period of important reevaluation of your internal spiritual and emotional needs and concepts, which will be very important in sustaining and, indeed, coping with the sudden growth and external change that will soon come about. Ideally, it should be a period of hard, goal-oriented work combined with an inner solidification that will enable you to hit the limelight with internal and external substance. At its worst, it can be a period of shiftless searching for real internal goals

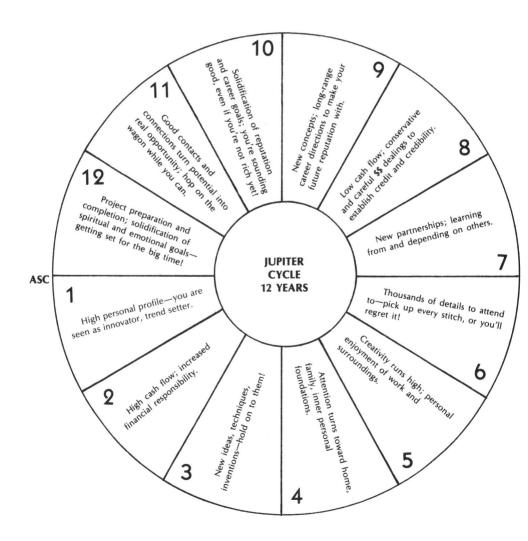

and some sort of tangible external source of income. The latter was the case with many of the "war babies" growing up in the sixties, who searched through that decade for spiritual reality through drugs and music and something meaningful to spend their lives doing. Many subsequently hit their No. 1 Jupiter cycle where everything blossomed for no apparent reason, and not a few proved totally incapable of handling the newfound success and either perished from drug abuse or vanished from sight after being unable to sustain the good fortune they were suddenly heirs to.

Those who survived have now repeated those same cycles in the late seventies and early eighties and perhaps they are the wiser for it. But without at least an intuitive understanding of the cyclic forces working on them, they may simply see another mystifying replay of the same ups and downs — except that this time there will be the creeping specter of middle age as the next frightening step.

This is not to suggest that understanding basic career and life cycles will give purpose or meaning to your life. There is no reason to believe it will. It does, however, remove a good deal of the mystery about your life and give you an overall structure upon which to base career activity, which then will have a chance to prove successful. Career success is not the answer to the cosmic riddle, but it sure beats career failure, and spiritual philosophy is much harder to come to grips with when you've got an empty stomach and no roof over your head.

JUPITER TABLE

1920: in Leo until August 27, into Virgo	**1939:** May 12, into Aries
	October 31, back into Pisces
1921: September 26, into Libra	December 21, forward into Aries
1922: October 27, into Scorpio	**1940:** May 17, into Taurus
1923: November 25, into Sagittarius	**1941:** May 27, into Gemini
1924: December 18, into Capricorn	**1942:** June 11, into Cancer
1925: In Capricorn all year	**1943:** July 1, into Leo
1926: January 6, into Aquarius	**1944:** July 13, into Virgo
1927: January 18, into Pisces	**1945:** August 26, into Libra
June 6, into Aries	**1946:** September 26, into Scorpio
September 11, back into Pisces	**1947:** October 25, into Sagittarius
1928: January 23, forward into Aries	**1948:** November 16, into Capricorn
June 4, into Taurus	**1949:** April 13, into Aquarius
1929: June 12, into Gemini	June 28, back into Capricorn
1930: June 27, into Cancer	December 1, forward into Aquarius
1931: July 18, into Leo	**1950:** April 16, into Pisces
1932: August 12, into Virgo	September 16, back into Aquarius
1933: September 11, into Libra	December 3, forward into Pisces
1934: October 12, into Scorpio	**1951:** April 22, into Aries
1935: November 10, into Sagittarius	**1952:** April 29, into Taurus
1936: December 3, into Capricorn	**1953:** May 10, into Gemini
1937: December 21, into Aquarius	**1954:** May 25, into Cancer
1938: May 15, into Pisces	**1955:** June 13, into Leo
July 31, back into Aquarius	November 18, into Virgo
December 30, forward into Pisces	

1956:   January 19, back into Leo
        July 8, forward into Virgo
        December 14, into Libra

1957:   January 20, back into Virgo
        August 8, forward into Libra

1958:   January 14, into Scorpio
        March 21, back into Libra
        September 8, forward into Scorpio

1959:   February 11, into Sagittarius
        April 25, back into Scorpio
        October 6, forward into Sagittarius

1960:   March 2, into Capricorn
        June 11, back into Sagittarius
        October 27, forward into Capricorn

1961:   March 16, into Aquarius
        August 13, back into Capricorn
        November 5, forward into Aquarius

1962:   March 26, into Pisces

1963:   April 5, into Aries

1964:   April 13, into Taurus

1965:   April 23, into Gemini
        September 22, into Cancer
        November 18, back into Gemini

1966:   May 6, forward into Cancer
        September 28, into Leo

1967:   January 17, back into Cancer
        May 24, forward into Leo
        October 20, into Virgo

1968:   February 28, back into Leo
        June 16, forward into Virgo
        November 16, into Libra

1969:   March 31, back into Virgo
        July 16, forward into Libra
        December 17, into Scorpio

1970:   May 1, back into Libra
        August 16, forward into Scorpio

1971:   January 24, into Sagittarius
        June 6, back into Scorpio
        September 12, forward into Sagittarius

1972:   February 7, into Capricorn
        July 25, back into Sagittarius
        September 26, forward into Capricorn

1973:   February 24, into Aquarius

1974:   March 9, into Pisces

1975:   March 19, into Aries

1976:   March 27, into Taurus
        August 24, into Gemini
        October 17, back into Taurus

1977:   April 4, forward into Gemini
        August 21, into Cancer
        December 31, back into Gemini

1978:   April 12, forward into Cancer
        September 6, into Leo

1979:   March 1, back into Cancer
        April 21, forward into Leo
        September 30, into Virgo

1980:   October 28, into Libra

1981:   November 28, into Scorpio

1982:   December 27, into Sagittarius

1983:   In Sagittarius all year

1984:   January 20, into Capricorn

1985:   February 7, into Aquarius

1986:   February 21, into Pisces

1987:   March 3, into Aries

1988:   March 8, into Taurus
        July 22, into Gemini
        December 1, back into Taurus

1989:   March 12, into Gemini
        July 31, into Cancer

1990:   August 19, into Leo

1991:   September 13, into Virgo

1992:   October 11, into Libra

1993:   November 11, into Scorpio

1994:   December 10, into Sagittarius

1995:   In Sagittarius

1996:   January 4, into Capricorn

1997:   January 22, into Aquarius

1998:   February 5, into Pisces

1999:   February 14, into Aries

2000:   February 15, into Taurus

5

SATURN:
CAREER PERIMETERS,
TESTING, AND SECURITY

The Saturn cycle of 29½ years is quite the opposite in effect of the Jupiter cycle, being a cycle of stress, testing, and forced economy—and the combination of the two cycles, as will be discussed in Chapter 7, has much to do with guiding the slings and arrows of outrageous fortune.

Just as Jupiter presented expansion and opportunity in each of its twelve separate cycles, Saturn has a damping and restricting effect that needs to be looked out for, but which need not be all bad. In fact, in the long run, it is the most securing and strengthening cycle of all if put to proper use. This is because it has the effect of forcing the individual to come to realistic terms with strengths and weaknesses in a given area and gets rid of a lot of chaff that tends to waste time, energy, and money. It teaches maximum economy of thought, motion, and goods so that in the future a little can go a lot longer than previously thought. If these lessons are studied and taken to heart, great benefit can be derived from periods that might otherwise seem like hard times. If they are ignored, the cycle of difficulties will simply repeat itself, only it will be harder the next time around.

The pursuit of any career is more than a series of landmark successes, as anyone knows. For most people, it is marked by long periods of drudgery and obscurity on the way to the top, if the top is ever reached. Sometimes the desired job cannot be secured and humdrum and futureless work has to be taken just to make ends meet. Still, there is no job so utterly boring and worthless that some profitable knowledge and experience cannot be gained from it. Consider it is just another necessary step in your career education. If you make the effort to do it well and glean all you can from it, you'll be better off later. And the duller and more profitless the job, the more you'll have to stretch your talents and imagination to get something out of it. That very ability to get something out of practically nothing—a hard exercise of the imagination and creativity—will measurably increase your powers and fundamental career horse sense. If, on the other hand, you wallow in your misery, you'll be weaker for it in the days to come and much less able to prevent yourself from falling on the same kind of hard luck again.

Saturn Cycle No. 1

As was the case with Jupiter, cycles No. 1 (when Saturn is on the Ascendant) and 2 (when it is in the next sign) are the most noticeable in terms of immediate career manifestations. They must be taken quite seriously and handled with patience and attention or they will have a very deleterious effect later on.

When Saturn is over the Ascendant, beginning its No. 1 cycle, it is usually a time of considerable personal stress, and the personality may be under fire from a number of quarters. The pressures are not primarily financial, though money may be involved, but have to do mainly with whether or not you can cut the mustard. Thus you may find yourself in a job that is somewhat over your head in terms of skills or personality and you must constantly struggle to live up to what is expected of you. Some people describe this 2½-year period as one in which you always feel as if you're walking around with a heavy weight on your shoulders. This is probably an appropriate description of the constant pressure and expectations that this cycle brings.

So what good can come of it? This cycle, by the time it is over, will give you a much clearer and more realistic view of your personal strengths and capabilities, and exercising them to the fullest during this time will hone them to a fine edge. Talents only blossom when you practice them, and this is a period of rigorous on-the-job training and relying on your wits.

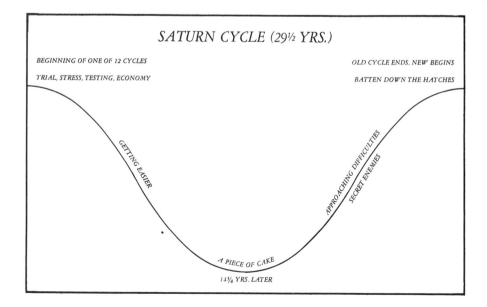

SATURN CYCLE (29½ YRS.)

BEGINNING OF ONE OF 12 CYCLES

TRIAL, STRESS, TESTING, ECONOMY

OLD CYCLE ENDS, NEW BEGINS

BATTEN DOWN THE HATCHES

GETTING EASIER

APPROACHING DIFFICULTIES

SECRET ENEMIES

A PIECE OF CAKE

14¾ YRS. LATER

The 192-hour week   Saturn cycle No. 1

Equally important, this period will educate you as to your real limits—you will find out just how far you can push yourself under fire before you can no longer make headway or you face collapse. To borrow an image from the recent hostilities in Southeast Asia, you will find out what your maximum effective perimeters are which can still withstand an all-out assault by the enemy.

In this regard, you will learn as much from your failures as from your successes, so do not allow yourself to become discouraged during this period. Instead, examine each failure and success in detail and find out just why they happened so that you may know how to prevent or repeat them in the future. You will come to depend on the knowledge you gain about your own abilities to withstand stress for the next 29½ years; and in many future situations that knowledge will mean the difference between success and failure.

So take advantage of the period and learn your lessons well. Here you are truly a student in the school of hard knocks, and its graduates are some of the most successful people in the world. In addition, you have the knowledge of the cyclical nature of the experience, so you should be one up on others who are not so fortunate and do not

"That one's from my Saturn period."

know when, if ever, this period is going to come to an end. Experience is the best teacher, as the saying goes, but you have to be willing to learn. The work you put in now, even though it won't have an immediate payoff, will be worth its weight in gold later on when this knowledge becomes a key to opportunity that your competitors lack.

Saturn Cycle No. 2

When Saturn has moved along into the next sign past your Ascendant, it enters its second cycle, and the focus of pressure and testing changes from personality to property and cash flow. Whereas previously you had to produce a maximum of effect from sheer personal power and talent, now you will have to learn to get a maximum amount of business done with a minimum of wherewithal. The chances are, whatever you're doing, you'll have to do it on a shoestring and try to make it look as if it was done on a fat budget.

This does not necessarily mean that you will be impoverished for the duration of this 2½-year period. Indeed, you may be rolling in dough if you're lucky, but the tasks

"I can always spot a man in a Saturn cycle."

you'll be asked to perform with it will be so monumental they will dwarf the available funds. Most people do experience a shortening of cash flow at this time, and if you aren't aware that it is just a phase that, like all others, will pass, it can get pretty scary when you look at diminishing funds accompanied by growing demands.

This can manifest itself in various ways. I know a woman in the organic cosmetics business who was offered some rare opportunities for growth and expansion during this period. But she was caught in a double-bind. In order to impress her potential buyers, who were very big in the industry, she had to dress like a million bucks and put on a show that would convince them she was an enormous success. That kind of "parading" is an unfortunate part of many businesses. She wasn't rich and successful—but she knew that she never would be if she didn't act as if she was.

So she mortgaged herself to the hilt and then begged, borrowed, and stole what she needed from every source she could dig up in order to put on the necessary showcase, using some rare and not entirely legal ingenuity. Thanks to applying her budget wizardry to the utmost, she got the clients and made back many times what she spent. And in the process, she learned how to get a lot more out of the dollar—she is not the spendthrift she once was. She was lucky. If the vagaries of fate had been entirely against her, she could have lost the clients and wound up bankrupt. But that isn't the

The big squeeze   Saturn cycle No. 2

dire fate it used to be in this society, and it would have taught her the limits of her budgeting talents. In either case, her future talents and skills would have been increased, guaranteeing her a better shot at success the next time.

On the other hand, if she had just given up or tried to make her pitch without the appropriate amount of show, she would have been out in the cold and would still be a very small-time businesswoman. Instead, she grasped the challenge of the No. 2 Saturn cycle and made a go of it. Even if she had lost, she would have been better off rising to the occasion than dropping the ball.

Whatever financial pressure you may find yourself under during this period, view it as a challenge to help you create better and more economical ways of getting things done. You may find that you can work miracles if you apply yourself, and you will certainly acquire habits and ways of managing funds that will save you incalculable amounts of money over the next 29½ years.

Saturn Cycle No. 3

Once the No. 2 cycle is over, the cash crunch will let up, albeit slowly at first. As Saturn passes into the third sign from the Ascendant, a new kind of pressure begins to be felt—pressure on the mind. This is not pressure of an emotional nature, but literally the necessity to produce the maximum mental output—plans, ideas, money-making schemes, and the like. It will force you to dig down to the bottom of the barrel for ideas that will be of profit to you, and your imagination will have to be stretched to the limit. It will be a trial of just how well you know the profession you have chosen and just how fast you can learn more about it as that becomes necessary.

The brain drain   Saturn cycle No. 3

If you have learned your job inside out, this need not be that difficult a period, except for the fact that you will be expected to regularly produce and demonstrate your knowledge of the field. If it is a field you like, this kind of work is really play.

The kind of knowledge you will be expected to demonstrate will be of a bare-bones, no-nonsense kind, so you will do well to spend a lot of time cutting away the chaff and delineating an unshakable position before you present your ideas. This period will test your ability to be succinct and tighten up your act where your mental powers are concerned.

The effect of this period will vary in intensity depending on your profession. For a writer, for instance, it is a very critical time, since the use of the mind is the primary function of that profession. I know one writer who, being aware of this cycle, did everything possible to refine and sharpen his already fairly laconic style during this period, paying particular attention to clarifying the logic of his expository writing. He spent as much time cleaning up and editing his work as in writing it in the first place, and these efforts established him firmly as a professional writer.

For professions that require less mental attention, such as some forms of athletics, this may be a much less critical time in terms of career, though it will doubtless have a strong effect on the mind. It will also, whatever your profession, cause you to trim social contacts that don't actually bring you money. In order to gain maximum clarity of thought, you need as much seclusion as possible to sort out your ideas and cook up new ones. This has the side effect of helping you separate your truly close friends from mere acquaintances who are time-wasters.

The third cycle is not so critical or pressured for most people as the first two, simply because the financial burden is usually alleviated, but it is an important period, particularly in regard to defining and refining career skills that will serve to support you and bring you more money in the future. To neglect doing this might not cause immediate loss, but it could well result in your being passed over later in favor of a competitor who was wiser in this respect than you were.

Saturn Cycle No. 4

The fourth Saturn cycle, when that planet is four signs from the Ascendant, begins a time of trial and pressure that is often more inner than outer in nature, though it can have considerable repercussions on your career. This seems to be a time when you have to come to terms with your relationships on the home front and learn how to balance and integrate them with your career aspirations. It will most frequently be a period of cutting back on heavier commitments at home until they are at a functional minimum in order to free you to do more at your job or career.

If you are single, this may mean moving away from your parents and relatives, or at least seriously cutting back contact with them. If you are married, it will mean more time at the office and less time at home, and you may experience real emotional conflict in carrying out these changes. It is housecleaning in the truest sense of the word, and the end result will be the preservation of those habits and commitments that are truly meaningful to you and the abandonment of customs that have become obligatory over the years but which serve no functional purpose except to impinge upon your time and money. Things like absolutely *having* to be at your parents' house for Thanksgiving, even if it shoots down an important sales trip. Or getting stuck fixing your husband's dinner, come hell or high water, no matter how rough a day you've had at the office. As the latter example indicates, this may be a particularly difficult period for career women, since society still seems to expect them to be glowing housewives even when they are holding down an exhausting executive position.

Even for those with relatively few family attachments, this is a period of 2½ years of household austerity or neglect. For many, home becomes simply a convenience for sleeping when they're in the neighborhood, and many an apartment has become a rundown mess during this time. If you get into this extreme state, you should do something to counteract it, as living quarters can do so much to buttress you for the day ahead if they're pleasant, and so much to depress you if they're not. In addition, in many professions the maintenance of a socially acceptable home (and often a family to go with it) is a must for getting ahead. This can make the fourth cycle an additional trial because your professional status may suffer as a result of what's going on at home.

If you spend some real time and energy coming to grips with these issues, you'll be far better off in the long run. The result will be an improved home climate that will be supportive rather than a burden, so that it actually serves to bolster your career efforts later on. If you neglect these issues, however, your home life will increasingly hinder your career, and unsettled problems with those dear to you may magnify into serious unhappiness, particularly when Saturn reaches its seventh cycle.

Saturn Cycle No. 5

As Saturn passes into the fifth sign past the Ascendant, you reach what might be termed a creativity crisis. You will likely find yourself in a spot where a good deal of spontaneous creativity is expected of you at a time when it doesn't come nearly as easily as it might. Aspects of your work that used to be easy and enjoyable now seem more like drudgery, yet they must be done anyway, and done well.

In professions such as music or the arts, where creativity is of the essence, this period can prove very difficult. I know one pop songwriter whose spontaneous creativity simply withered on the vine at this time. He had always relied on music and lyrics to just spring up from his fertile brain, but all of a sudden his brain was barren ground. This could have spelled the end of his career, and I know others in the same line of work for whom it has. Fortunately, he was determined to keep going by whatever method necessary, and he developed a whole new approach to his craft. He began to analyze the structure of current hit song styles, musically and lyrically— something not all that difficult, since this was the early disco era. This approach allowed him to fabricate a marketable song on a purely technical basis, without having to rely on inspiration from the muse. In addition, he picked up a writing partner who was not going through the same cycle to add the needed spontaneity. Thus he not only survived the period financially, but he kept his career and picked up a valuable self-imposed music education as well.

I know of another case of an actress who found her Method acting style failed her during this cycle. The only way out was to learn more traditional styles that didn't depend so much on inspiration. This tactic saw her through and immensely broadened her scope and talents as an actress.

The fickle muse   Saturn cycle No. 5

Another side effect of this lack of inspiration can be a considerably diminished sex life, which can take its toll on your career energies. The old animal magnetism seems to wane during these 2½ years—and when spontaneity doesn't come easily, you're just not as sexy as usual. Rather than fight an uphill battle, one you really won't win even if you do achieve nominal success, it's a lot easier on the psyche to just write off the whole subject for the duration and sublimate those energies into career matters where they may do the most good.

By the time the fifth cycle is over, if you have used it to the fullest, you will have a much firmer structure for your innate creativity when it returns, whatever your profession, because you will have actively survived a period where you had to get along without it. Creativity will be henceforth a force that you can mold and control. If, however, you drift aimlessly through this period, creativity will be something that comes mysteriously out of thin air—and whenever the muse decides to desert you, you've had it.

Saturn Cycle No. 6

Once Saturn goes into the sixth sign from your Ascendant (remember, the Ascendant sign counts as No. 1), you move into a period of particularly plain hard work. This is a real testing period for your basic business and trade skills, particularly those of a detailed, noncreative nature. Your work load increases, and though your creativity is returning, you won't find much use for it. The most important activity to see you through this period is knuckling down and putting your nose to the grindstone.

If this period last occurred for you during high school or college, you probably experienced it as a time when subjects were particularly tough and required a lot more routine study to get through. If you had been coasting before, it made things doubly bad, because your skills weren't up to par. The same is true in the business world, and this is a testing period of your ability to stay on top of all the details. And that ability depends largely on how well you utilized your last Jupiter sixth cycle.

This is, in fact, a general principle of career cycles, which will be dealt with in depth in Chapter 7. Where Jupiter cycles have not been used well or have been wasted, the equivalent Saturn cycle will be particularly difficult. Where Saturn cycles have been wasted, the equivalent Jupiter cycles will not bring nearly so much gain.

A good example is a hardware distributor I know. The hardware business is a very detailed one, in which you literally have to know every nut and bolt. During his Jupiter sixth cycle he was faced with a flurry of details and invoices as his formerly small hardware store began to expand. Being a person who enjoyed picking up every stitch, he spent day and night keeping things in excellent order, a job that might have frustrated someone less meticulous.

By the time Saturn got around to the same place, he had established such a good track record that he was able to sell his store and take over the much more difficult but higher-paying job of major distributor. Had he attempted such a task coming out of a weak Jupiter sixth cycle, it would have proved too much for him and he would have been swamped. But he had done his homework, so to speak, and the testing period of the Saturn sixth cycle proved him more than fit for the task and made him piles of money to boot.

Therefore, if you are approaching a Saturn sixth cycle, look back on your last Jupiter sixth and see how well you handled that (reread that relevant part of Chapter 4 if you're in doubt). That will give you a clue as to how pleasant or unpleasant the coming Saturn sixth cycle will be—whether it will be sheer misery or a period of hard but profitable work.

Saturn Cycle No. 7

As Saturn completes half of its total Ascendant cycle and is in the seventh sign from the Ascendant, you will find yourself in a period of housecleaning as far as your partners in business and personal life are concerned. This is a period in which you will establish just how much you are willing to take from them and what the boundaries concerning privileges should be. Frequently it is a time of separation from exploitative colleagues or hangers-on who don't pull their weight. You may acquire a new partner or stabilize a partnership that is working out well—in fact, this is a period for all sorts of partnership deals.

For example, a publisher I know went into this cycle with nagging doubts about his partner, who really wasn't doing very much to help the business. But he was an old friend, so the publisher was reluctant to split with him. Finally the pressure became so intense—his wife was taking on much of the work his partner should have been doing—that he decided, old friend or not, his partner had to go for the sake of the business, which was beginning to suffer badly. So he bought out his partner and installed his wife as co-publisher, and business picked up again soon after. In one fell swoop he got rid of the chaff and cemented a professional relationship with someone who had been around in an unofficial capacity for a long time.

Things don't always work out so neatly or quickly, however. You may find yourself having to choose between going it alone for a while or sticking with someone who is holding you back or making operations more difficult or inefficient. Remember,

Partner perplex   Saturn cycle No. 7

if you don't take the opportunity at this time, the chances are you'll be stuck for God knows how long with an albatross around your neck. Essentially this is a negative opportunity that will have positive effects at a later date.

Sometimes this partner-trimming effect is felt more in your personal life, resulting in separations, break-ups, or divorces when individuals finally decide they've had enough. As in the business, it may also entail the firming up of a relationship with a potential marriage partner.

Even where the effect does not fall directly in the profeesional sphere, it will have repercussions there, draining a certain amount of energy that might ordinarily be exerted in professional relationships. Ultimately, I think the personal side is more important, but in the short run it could really hurt your bank account.

Saturn Cycle No. 8

As Saturn moves into the eighth sign from the Ascendant, you move into a period during which the main issue of struggle and controversy in your life may turn out to be credit, or at least the use of other people's money and resources. The chances are you will need to rely on these, and the care you exercise here may have a good deal to do with your future credit rating and money-handling reputation. If you are meticulous in repaying loans and only use the money for what you say you will, you will establish an irreproachable reputation, which will serve you well in later efforts to gain extra financing. This is doubly important, because loans of any size may be particularly hard to get at this time, and any previous carelessness (such as when money wasn't so tight back in your last Jupiter eighth cycle) could make things even harder. Still, even in such a case, this is an ideal period for reestablishing credibility.

A carpenter I know who had a so-so credit rating, but didn't really need a good one since he was doing relatively well, took this opportunity to change things around. He took out a small loan he didn't really need and then paid it back rather rapidly. He continued along this way, buying things on time wherever he could, but paying back early to save the interest. He established credit with all his suppliers, and after a couple of years he had a magnificent credit rating, despite the fact that he had very little in substantive property such as houses, stocks, or bonds. A year or so later he was able to borrow heavily when an opportunity to become a contractor came along. Had he not taken the time and trouble to establish an excellent credit rating, he would have had to pass up the chance of a lifetime.

On the other hand, I know a veterinarian who is quite wealthy (he owns several offices and a number of prime Manhattan buildings) but can't even get an American Express Card. Why? Because he doesn't pay his bills on time and doesn't like to borrow. He just won't pay the pound of flesh, in terms of interest, that it takes to get credit. The sad fact is that banks have to make a good deal of interest off you before they'll give you much of a credit rating. That's how New York City got so heavily into debt—it was willing to get ripped off by the banks at the highest loan rates paid by any city in the country.

The chances are slim that you'll go through anything that extreme, but the eighth cycle is generally a time when you feel pressure concerning the way you use other people's money, whether in the form of a loan or in the carrying out of your job responsibilities with funds or property belonging to a company or individual. If you handle small matters well, the opportunities for larger responsibilities will grow. If you slip up, then it's small potatoes for a long time to come.

Saturn Cycle No. 9

When Saturn swings into the ninth sign from your Ascendant, you are likely to find yourself in a time of conceptual crystalization of a very broad life-directional sort that can have a profound effect on your future. This will often be a time when you reject many of the goals you previously set and clarify for yourself goals you now see as more meaningful. The result could be changed career, social status, possessions, family, and spiritual beliefs, so it is not a period to go through lightly.

During this period I have seen straight businessmen turn into flower children and hippies transform themselves into hard-nosed shopkeepers. It is a time of coming to terms with one's overall beliefs, and that is bound to seriously affect one's career.

For example, a doctor I know who was raking in a bundle in a very lucrative high-class specialized practice began to have doubts about he value of his life during this period. He was making a lot of money, but he was doing very little to fulfill his medical vows about helping humanity. In fact, he spent most of his time fixing up corns, bunions, and other more specialized foot diseases, mostly in the infirm rich. He considered giving it all up and becoming a general practitioner in some out-of-the-way town that really needed him—but that would waste most of his specialized knowledge and destroy his family's standard of living. After much personal agonizing, he was lucky enough to stumble on a compromise: He continued a somewhat diminished practice and began devoting as much time as he could to a program of research and development of artificial legs and feet, a pair of which may someday adorn the first real Bionic Man. Thus he was able to make a real contribution without doing too much damage to his income or lifestyle.

Not everyone is given the opportunity to play both ends against the middle philosophically and succeed at it. Often the change is radical and will significantly alter the nature of the career, making the following No. 10 cycle a time of real struggle and intense effort to become established in a new way.

Probably as important as the career effects of this period are its moral implications. Jobs may come and go, but it is inner convictions and one's ability to live up to them that make life worth living or a hollow routine. It is wise to wait until all those questions have been successfully grappled with—the lifestyle you really want and its effects on your inner life, the outside world, and those you care for—before too drastically altering your career direction. It is tempting to go with quick answers that may be deeply regretted later.

Before you toss a promising career in the ditch, think hard and make sure your new direction is one you can stick with, because you will need all the conviction at your command to make it workable in the approaching cycle.

Saturn Cycle No. 10

As Saturn moves into the tenth sign past your Ascendant, whatever conceptual changes you have gone through during the ninth cycle you will now have to bring to bear in your career to achieve a reputation for implementing them. Since they are so interrelated, the chances are their mutual effects will tend to blend over a 5-year period instead of being sharply delineated into two 2½-year periods. During the No. 10 part of this blend, however, the emphasis will be increasingly on carving out a niche for yourself in the world, not always in agreement with your earlier directions or those you were involved with then. Therefore, you will have a doubly difficult time of it because you will lack the support you previously had at a time when you don't have the experience in new areas to be effectively independent. During this period you may feel you're out in the cold with nothing but your convictions to keep you warm.

Applied ingenuity should see you through. A lot also depends upon what Jupiter cycles you are going through during this period. If Jupiter is in a particularly supportive cycle financially, such as the No. 2, and you are paying close attention to handling it well, then the Saturn No. 10 should be a lot easier to bear. If Jupiter is in its No. 6 cycle, however, you might find yourself inundated with more chores that you can handle without sufficient financial and reputational support. It all depends on where the two cycles began at your birth and how many turns they have had time for. If this sounds a bit like career roulette, it is, except that you must remember that these are simply cycles of *influence* and it is your *personal resolve* and use of them that will determine the outcome in the end.

For many of the innocent younger flower children of the late sixties, the No. 9-No. 10 cycle represented the tremendous struggle, first conceptual and then financial, to leave the dying world of the dropout and enter the depressed economy of the early seventies that was less than receptive to such intruders. These people had to come to terms with a hastily conceived dropout philosophy, and many found themselves running back to college or jumping with both feet into essentially standard forms of sales and commerce. The transition was harder, since they were latecomers, but the booming business in boutiques, "head" paraphernalia, and other "new age" commercialism is testament to their general success.

Conversely, for the next-older generation (by 5 years or so), the trauma of changed self-commitment wasn't the exit from the sixties, but the entrance, when they had to rework the unrealistic and dehumanizing goals of the fifties. It was their struggle that established the "new age" concepts of today, while the struggle of the following group was to turn those concepts into cash and make them acceptable facts of life within the social context. Many of the earlier generation's contributions became watered down in the process, but many also became more practical and therefore more useful than they could have been in their original form.

Perhaps the current struggle in this area may be the attempt to integrate the recent diverse branching and discoveries of the spiritual world with the necessities of the business world. Much change for the good may come of that synthesis, but it will not be an easy one.

Saturn Cycle No. 11

As Saturn passes into the eleventh sign past the Ascendant, a period of marked independence, from both the giving and receiving of career aid, generally sets in. If your previous struggles have been a success, it is because you eschewed the help of those now-jealous superiors who so recently opposed you and said you'd never make it. If you haven't succeeded, it's because successes don't like to associate with failures.

In this period you cannot count on much help from higher-ups. Sometimes the reason is an innocent one you don't suspect and may not find out about until later. For instance, I knew one record producer in the sixties who was quite talented and was producing records that really fit into the pop sound of the time. But for some reason, during this No. 11 cycle he couldn't get any of the big record companies to buy them for release. He would take the product to a major company representative, who would praise it and say what big hit potential it had, but then as things progressed, interest would wane and the whole thing would fall through. He couldn't understand what was wrong—until the kickback scandal caused the big companies to completely alter the way they chose their products. Then he realized what his error had been: He hadn't offered the company representatives a kickback from the company advance they were supposed to give him!

Such remarkable innocence is seldom found among record producers these days, but a hundred other things could keep higher-ups from smiling on you during this No. 11 cycle, and they could escape your notice until long afterward. But if we all had to depend on handouts from those more fortunate, we'd be in pretty bad shape, so this period has the distinct advantage of teaching independence and forcing you to rely on yourself when there is no one around to help you out.

Related to this effect is the fact that those you can rely on during this period will be friends indeed, and not simply companions of convenience. This tends to be a time when you find out who your real friends are—and aren't. When cut off from superiors, you discover which of your equals base their decisions on personal attachment and which let money and convenience determine their alliances.

Whether you are more likely to remain at your current level or rise up the ladder of success because of your independence again may be largely affected by Jupiter's cycle position. A No. 1 cycle for Jupiter would do much to provide an upward thrust, while, say, a No. 7 cycle would tend to keep you among your equals.

Saturn Cycle No. 12

As Saturn makes its final move before returning to the point and sign of your Ascendant, you may find yourself going through a particularly treacherous period in which you will do well to watch your step. This is a time when your efforts to get ahead may easily be subverted without your knowledge by those who have your interests least at heart. Thus you may find yourself quite undeservingly held back and not know how to alter the situation.

For example, a friend of mine was an excellent accountant at a major firm in New York. She was next in line for head accountant, and when her superior left for another company, she was overjoyed. She just knew she was going to get the job—she had the qualifications and the seniority, as well as ample experience with that particular firm's officers who would make the appointment.

But she was in a No. 12 Saturn cycle and her expectations were not destined to be fulfilled. Instead, the president of the firm overrode the recommendations of his

Some of your best friends   Saturn cycle No. 12

advisers and appointed another woman from outside the firm with far less to recommend her—except that she was his mistress. My friend was crushed, and immediately resigned her position and sought work in another firm—quite the right decision since a company with management that fickle is not a safe place to be. Unfortunately, it took her much too long to find that out, and the discovery was painful when it came. Knowledge of the twelfth cycle might not have prevented what happened, but it certainly would have softened the blow.

It is a good idea to keep very careful records of all agreements during this period, particularly in areas where you might normally be a little lax such as in handshake agreements with friends and the like. Trouble may be brewing even among your nearest and dearest, so don't be unnecessarily trusting. I've seen it happen a number of times, and the first and most painful time was when a very close friend and business associate deliberately stabbed me in the back, something I found was in the making for most of the Saturn No. 12 cycle I had just finished. All my most important agreements with him had been basically verbal or insufficiently documented, and what followed was a hopeless and bitter dispute that I could not possibly hope to win. Had I been more prudent earlier, I would at least have had a leg to stand on, but I had never figured him for a traitor—but then, that can be said about all successful traitors.

The key to understanding this sometimes puzzling period is that coming up next is the No. 1 cycle of personality trial and testing, and that the trials of tomorrow must already be brewing somewhere. Your duty, therefore, is to cover yourself wherever you can, a basic and invaluable technique that everyone in business must learn to get ahead (or keep from falling behind), and which will be discussed at greater length in the last chapter of this book.

This concept of getting ready for the next cycle ahead of time is one of the primary uses of this book. By knowing the kind of general influences that are in the offing, you can set your sails ahead of time and save yourself a lot of scrambling in an unexpected gale. Those unfamiliar with career cycles will not necessarily perish—after all, merchant fleets managed to survive before the advent of weather forecasting. The main elements of success are the sturdiness of the ship and the skill and determination of the captain and crew. Still, most people these days check the weather report before venturing far out onto the open sea.

Basically, the interaction of Jupiter and Saturn cycles sets the main patterns for career direction, just as the earth's orbital cycle and the sun's emission cycles set the general weather patterns on the planet—but there are other important factors to be taken into consideration before rushing to any conclusions or predictions. Some of them will be discussed in the following chapters.

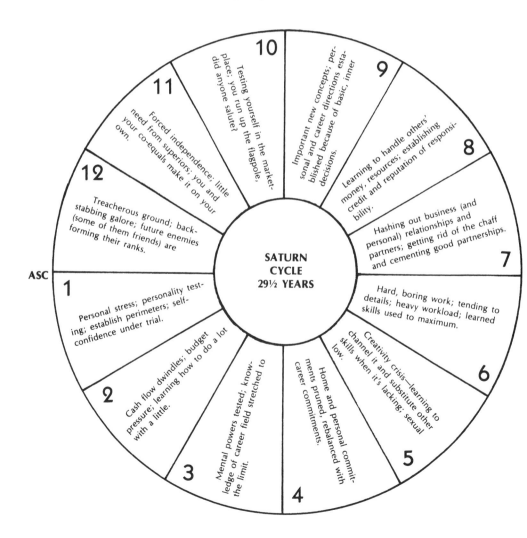

SATURN CYCLE 29½ YEARS

ASC

10 — Testing yourself in the market-place; you run up the flagpole, did anyone salute?

11 — Forced independence; little need from superiors; you and your co-equals make it on your own.

12 — Treacherous ground; back-stabbing galore; future enemies (some of them friends) are forming their ranks.

9 — Important new concepts; personal and career directions established because of basic, inner decisions.

8 — Learning to handle others' money, resources; establishing credit and reputation of responsibility.

7 — Hashing out business (and personal) relationships and partners; getting rid of the chaff and cementing good partnerships.

1 — Personal stress; personality testing; establish perimeters; self-confidence under trial.

2 — Cash flow dwindles; budget pressure; learning how to do a lot with a little.

3 — Mental powers tested; knowledge of career field stretched to the limit.

6 — Hard, boring work; tending to details; heavy workload; learned skills used to maximum.

5 — Creativity crisis—learning to channel it and substitute other skills when it's lacking; sexual low.

4 — Home and personal commitments pruned, rebalanced with career commitments.

SATURN TABLE

1920:	In Virgo all year
1921:	October 8, into Libra
1922:	In Libra
1923:	December 20, into Scorpio
1924:	April 6, back into Libra
	September 14, into Scorpio
1925:	In Scorpio
1926:	December 3, into Sagittarius
1927:	In Sagittarius
1928:	In Sagittarius
1929:	March 15, into Capricorn
	May 5, back into Sagittarius
	November 30, into Capricorn
1930:	In Capricorn
1931:	In Capricorn
1932:	February 24, into Aquarius
	August 14, back into Capricorn
	November 20, into Aquarius
1933:	In Aquarius
1934:	In Aquarius
1935:	February 15, into Pisces
1936:	In Pisces
1937:	April 26, into Aries
	October 19, back into Pisces
1938:	January 15, into Aries
1939:	July 7, into Taurus
	September 23, back into Aries
1940:	March 21, into Taurus
1941:	In Taurus
1942:	May 9, into Gemini
1943:	In Gemini
1944:	June 21, into Cancer
1945:	In Cancer
1946:	August 3, into Leo
1947:	In Leo
1948:	September 20, into Virgo
1949:	April 4, back into Leo
	May 30, into Virgo
1950:	In Virgo
1951:	August 14, into Libra
1952:	In Libra
1953:	October 23, into Scorpio
1954:	In Scorpio
1955:	In Scorpio
1956:	January 13, into Sagittarius
	May 15, back into Scorpio
	October 11, into Sagittarius
1957:	In Sagittarius
1958:	In Sagittarius
1959:	January 6, into Capricorn
1960:	In Capricorn

1961:	In Capricorn
1962:	January 3, into Aquarius
1963:	In Aquarius
1964:	March 25, into Pisces
	September 17, back into Aquarius
	December 17, into Pisces
1965:	In Pisces
1966:	In Pisces
1967:	March 4, in Aries
1968:	In Aries
1969:	April 30, into Taurus
1970:	In Taurus
1971:	June 19, into Gemini
1972:	January 11, back into Taurus
	February 22, into Gemini
1973:	In Gemini
1974:	April 19, into Cancer
1975:	September 18, into Leo
1976:	January 15, back into Cancer
	June 6, into Leo
1977:	November 18, into Virgo
1978:	January 5, back into Leo
	July 26, into Virgo
1979:	In Virgo
1980:	September 22, into Libra
1981:	In Libra
1982:	November 30, into Scorpio
1983:	May 7, back into Libra
	August 25, into Scorpio
1984:	In Scorpio
1985:	November 18, into Sagittarius
1986:	In Sagittarius
1987:	In Sagittarius
1988:	February 16, into Capricorn
	June 11, back into Sagittarius
	November 13, into Capricorn
1989:	In Capricorn
1990:	In Capricorn
1991:	February 7, into Aquarius
1992:	In Aquarius
1993:	May 22, into Pisces
	July 1, back into Aquarius
1994:	January 29, into Pisces
1995:	In Pisces
1996:	April 8, into Aries
1997:	In Aries
1998:	June 10, into Taurus
	October 26, back into Aries
1999:	March 2, into Taurus
2000:	August 11, into Gemini
	October 17, back into Taurus

Progress Report

Stop! Don't go any further without reading this. Otherwise, chances are you will have wasted the bread you shelled out for this book.

Like most curious souls, you have probably been looking back on your own history as you read the last few chapters, particularly those on Jupiter and Saturn, and saying, "That's exactly what happened to me," or "It didn't happen that way at all." Worse, you might be thinking, upon looking at what's coming up, "Lord, things were looking pretty good and now I'm going to have to face *that*?"

Well, first of all, the whole picture isn't painted yet. There are ameliorating factors to be filled in that can vastly change parts of the scenario.

Second, you may even be making some rudimentary but common mistakes both in the calculation of your cycles and in judging the nature of cycles themselves. Now is the time to correct that, before things get more complex. Here's a list of checkpoints:

1. Do you have your correct birth time? Are you sure?
2. Did you correct it for Daylight Savings or War Time?
3. Did you add your total correctly (hours and minutes are in 60s, not 100s)?
4. Did your Ascendant fall very early or very late in a sign (see note on Ascendant Worksheet in Chapter 2)? This can change the years where the cycles fall by 6 months for Jupiter and 1 year or more for Saturn.
5. Did you read your Ascendant off the correct latitude table?

If you've got all these bases covered, then the chances are any discrepancies will be resolved by the factors discussed in the next chapter.

There's one other possibility, however, which also applies to the "wild card" factors in the next chapter: It is the nature of cycles themselves. They are not fixed, relentless circles that move without change or variation. Rather, for environmental reasons down here, and because of varying retrogradation up there, they may stray from their allotted average positions. This is particularly the case in the fourth and tenth cycles, and to a lesser extent in those immediately surrounding them. There is little or no variation around the first and seventh cycles.

Therefore, you may spot a trend in your past as much as a year or so off in the varying areas. Where you do, remember it and figure that it is likely to repeat itself next cycle and adjust accordingly. The idea of this book is to spot *your* repeating cycles, not those of a statistical mass of study cases. Each of us is unique, so we don't respond to even the most fixed cycles exactly the same as another.

For this reason also, let the past be your instructor. Whenever your experience with a given cycle varies from the common interpretation, add your personal shading before applying the interpretation to your future. You will have a much better idea of what is coming up.

Now go on and read the rest of the book.

6

THE "WILD CARDS": URANUS, NEPTUNE, AND PLUTO

Although all cycles are regular, by definition, there are points at which any given cycle may be broken, interrupted, or suppressed. This can occur in nature, for instance, for various reasons. A freak set of weather conditions may interrupt a migration cycle, or even stop it entirely until the following year, at which time it will reestablish itself.

In some cases, such as sunspot cycles, the interruption may occur for a much longer period of time for reasons that are so far unknown. During the period from 1645 to 1715, which astronomers call the "Maunder minimum" after the man who researched it, there were hardly any sunspots at all, causing a radical climate change called the "Little Ice Age." But in 1715 the cycle resumed and we have not seen another major interruption since, though some say one is due. There were earlier interruptions: between 1460 and 1550 (called the "Sporer minimum") and between 1100 and 1250, (called the "Grand maximum"), when there was a tremendous surge of sunspot activity roughly coinciding with the Crusades. But after each of these interruptions the normal cycle was reestablished.

Regular cycles can also be suppressed by other, interfering cycles. Wild-hare population cycles are known to be suppressed by the longer fox population cycle peak. As long as there are an unusually large number of foxes around to gobble them up, the hares just can't make it to their normal peak population. When the foxes decrease in number, according to their normal cycle, the hares reestablish their own population cycle.

The regular career cycles of Jupiter and Saturn have their own special brand of "foxes" that regularly suppress or interrupt their effects. These are the cycles of the planets Uranus, Neptune, and Pluto, which are far longer than the cycles of Jupiter and Saturn and tend to interfere with the effects of these two main career cycles. Depending upon the planet involved, the Jupiter or Saturn cycle period may become much more chaotic and unpredictable, or its effects may be so diffused or held down as to be barely noticeable. It is, of course, important to know when these unfortunate interruptions will occur, as it could be disastrous to get all wound up for a lot of new energy (as with Jupiter) and find that nothing happens. Similarly with Saturn, the period of stress you are expecting could turn out to be twice as difficult as you had anticipated.

Because of the long cycles of these planets, you will only experience their effects in a few specific areas where they interfere with the shorter cycles, but their effects are quite strong and can really throw you off your stride if you're unprepared. Indeed, even when they do not directly interfere, they can color the interaction of the Jupiter and Saturn cycles (this will be discussed in the next chapter).

Uranus

The cycle of Uranus is 84 years, so if you are lucky you will live to see a complete one. Because of the proportionate differences in length, Uranus will interfere with Jupiter in roughly every third sign position, at 14-year intervals, while interfering with Saturn every sixth sign, at 45-year intervals.

Whenever Jupiter or Saturn appears in the same sign as Uranus (check the Table of Outer Planets and Lunar Nodes), your personal cycle of Jupiter or Saturn will be upset accordingly. The effect of Uranus is to turn a normal situation into sporadic chaos and unexpected change. In the case of either Jupiter or Saturn, this can foul things up unless you are extra careful to keep your balance and expect the unexpected. Forewarned in such a situation, you may be able to keep your head when others around you are not able to, giving you a decided advantage.

A printer I know underwent a difficult period, providing us with a necessarily negative example of this cycle brought on by the last conjunction of Jupiter and Uranus in late 1969. His Ascendant was in Virgo, so the Uranus cycle ran right into his No. 2 Jupiter cycle, one sign away in Libra. True to form, the No. 2 Jupiter cycle was bringing him greater cash flow and business was going especially well. Thanks to Uranus's interference, however, the "flow" was more like an intermittent series of spurts. Thus, when he got sudden large last-minute orders, he didn't have the ability to handle them. Then, afterward, there would be a long period of no orders at all, at which time his overhead nearly broke him. The result was that other printers not experiencing this sporadic, if voluminous, business, gradually overtook him and he was eventually forced to sell the business. Had he known what was in store, perhaps he could have arranged his employee schedule so that he would have a lot of help when it was needed and not be stuck with a large payroll when it wasn't. It simply never occurred to him because the problem wasn't happening to other printers around him—it was a situation unique to him, and it put him out of business.

Similarly, when Uranus interferes with Jupiter in any of its cycles, this same kind of upset and jangling effect may be observed. This No. 4 cycle is normally a time of home-moving, expansion, or relocation, but with Uranus there, such events may happen not once but several times and without warning. Therefore, any move at that time should be made with caution, lest the expense of another unexpected one break the bank account.

It is more difficult to say exactly what the interference of Uranus with the Saturn cycle means, but enough observations have been made of its influence upon the Jupiter-Saturn cycle relationship (a cycle of 20 years) to hazard a guess. Probably the effect

Uranus

of Saturn and Uranus cycles together is to very much exaggerate the clarity and crystallizing effect of a normal Saturn cycle. Whereas the Saturn cycle tends to be one of testing and bringing everything down to basics, the influence of Uranus will add extra clarity and help form rules of action and behavior that will last and be effective for much longer than normally might be anticipated.

SPECIAL NOTE:

If you're beginning to get dizzy from the various cycles and numbers being bandied about, relief is only a chapter away. Everything covered so far can be set down in the most deceptively easy graph forms, which will be described in Chapter 7. Exactly how and where the effects of Uranus, Neptune, and Pluto change the overall career cycles will be much easier to discern on a year-to-year basis using the graphs, but don't skip the rest of this chapter. If you don't know the basic qualities of these "wild card" planets and their cycles, reading the graphs won't help you. If necessary, just ignore all the cycle period numbers here (they're for math and astronomy enthusiasts) and stick to the meanings. Where they all interact will be eminently clear later.

Neptune

Where Neptune interferes with a Jupiter and Saturn cycle (where it's in the same sign), its effect is one of diffusion and uncertainty. It tends to muddy the waters of a normally clear cycle and make it more difficult to comprehend and utilize. Unlike Uranus, whose interference occurs relatively rarely, Neptune interferes with Jupiter every 13 years, in successive cycle numbers, and with Saturn every 35 years, usually in the same cycle number. Thus, once in each total round of Jupiter and Saturn, Neptune will interfere in very close to the same place. That will tend to become a depressed period for learning and opportunity and should be given special attention to make up for it.

When coinciding with a Jupiter cycle, Neptune is frequently deceptively exhilarating. Take the example of a friend of mine who opened a "head" shop and began developing a line of products with which to supply it back in 1971 when that industry was still a small one. He has an Ascendant in Gemini, so he was going through a No. 7 Jupiter cycle at the time (it was in Sagittarius, where Neptune also was). He was a bit underfunded, so he was glad when several wealthier smoking buddies offered to chip in and become partners. Considering the cycle, this was a logical time to hook up with new people. But instead of carefully going over the contracts to see that they were fair to all concerned, he just signed what was put before him, trusting the "good vibes." Everybody was mellow and stoned, so what could go wrong? Well, for my friend, everything could—and did. When he woke up from his smoke-filled haze about a year later, he found himself a junior partner in his own firm and well on the irreversible road to being put out on the street. In hindsight, the contract he had signed was sheer financial suicide, and by 1973 he was forced out of the business entirely.

What could he have done if he had known about either Jupiter's or Neptune's effects at the time? Well, he still would have been ripe for deceiving, but at least he could have gotten the advice of a good lawyer and not been taken for a complete ride. Or he could have chosen to remain small and taken the opportunity to develop when things became a little clearer during the next Jupiter cycle. The fact is, there isn't always a lot you *can* do to overcome the damping effect of the "wild card" planet cycles, except to wait out the storm and launch yourself later in clearer weather. I hope that in 1984, when Neptune interferes with my friend's No. 8 cycle (in Capricorn), that he will refrain from handling credit or other people's money too loosely or he will find himself in similar ruin. In fact, perhaps the wisest idea would be to choose a good money-managing

Neptune

partner (now that he'll be more careful about *that* kind of choice) and stay out of the whole area as much as possible until Jupiter moves on.

The interaction of Neptune with a Saturn cycle hasn't happened since 1952, but I do have a good example, sort of by accident. A rather embittered person in the women's rights movement told me the story (her own), and it fits the principles concerned. Her Ascendant is in Taurus, and she graduated law school in 1952, when she was just entering her No. 6 Saturn cycle. At the time she had the misfortune to accept a (very) junior partnership in an otherwise all-male law firm, under the impression that if she worked extra hard she could nullify disadvantages of status and sex and rise to the top along with her colleagues who had graduated at the same time.

She couldn't have been more wrong. Not only was she in a period (Saturn No. 6) when she would have to pick up every stitch and show maximum expertise—something she was much too inexperienced to do successfully—but the Neptune influence led to even more confusion and error. Before long she found her duties those of a secretary. And thanks to the collusive and mostly male nature of the legal profession at that time, there was little chance of her getting any better status at another firm if she decided to move.

The result was she decided to quit the profession rather than go through life as a glorified girl Friday, and seemingly all of her years of law study had thus been wasted. Actually, as it turned out, that wasn't the case because her background in law led her into consumer advocacy and the women's movement after a few years of kicking around the business world, and she has been able to make a very real and creative contribution as a result. But this was only after years of pain, rejection, and disappointment, which have very much left their mark on her soul.

How could she have avoided it? That is a very difficult question to answer, since even the Jupiter cycle was sucking her into that ill-fated decision to join the law firm. Jupiter was over her Ascendant in the No. 1 cycle, making her look and feel like she was rarin' to go and would make a sure success of things. On all sides circumstances were pulling her toward a disastrous decision. Within the options available to her, probably joining the Legal Aid Society would have been the best—that being the least favored kind of job at the time, she would have had the easiest competition to battle and the Jupiter cycle would have done more to help, since she would have been appearing in public more. But taking such a lowly position after struggling through an expensive, high-class law school would never have occurred to her. There are many times, particularly when "wild card" planets interfere, when the safest thing is to stay put or even seemingly regress, rather than walk right into a swamp that, in the name of progress, may spell doom for your career. Decisions like that are painful to make, but it is just as well to have the extra career cycle information at hand before making them.

Pluto

Where Pluto interferes with the Jupiter and Saturn cycles it usually has the effect of heavily suppressing them (in the case of Jupiter) or making them particularly oppressive (in the case of Saturn). It will usually affect the same area repeatedly or move on one cycle farther at the most, so it will lend focus to what will be a definite problem area in the career realm. Indeed, when that planet is passing within a couple of degrees or so of the Ascendant, career success seems to be virtually impossible. Thus, recently, those with middle or late Libra Ascendants have been taking a terrible beating careerwise— something I can offer no explanation for, outside of traditional astrological lore that depicts Pluto as the planet of death and transformation and has very little good to say of it.

At any rate, you may find that whatever Jupiter or Saturn cycle this planet affects will be depressed, meaning that you'll get a lot less good out of a Jupiter cycle and a lot more difficulty out of a Saturn cycle.

An example of Jupiter cycle suppression comes from a woman who was in the jewelry business, making and selling her own designs. Her Ascendant is late in Virgo, so when Jupiter was there in 1968 her No. 1 cycle occurred and she should have gotten quite a boost out of it. Unfortunately, Pluto was also hovering in that spot, and no matter how vigorous a selling job she did, she couldn't get any buyers, despite the excellent quality of her work. Normally, at this time she should have looked even better than she really was, but thanks to Pluto quite the opposite happened. Everyone turned her down, and she was really distraught, not understanding why her efforts were meeting with total failure.

Lacking any buyers, she decided to produce her jewelry herself, hoping that bit by bit she could build up a business and let the public decide on their own whether her jewelry designs were any good. As she went into her following No. 2 Jupiter cycle, that's just what did happen and she found she couldn't keep up with the demand. Before

Pluto

long she had her own flourishing small company, so she just said to hell with trying to impress buyers. Thanks to her perseverance, the Pluto damping effect wound up doing her more good than harm—because she decided to sidestep it rather than battle on against impossible odds.

This, in fact, is the key to handling the interference of the three "wild card" planets with Jupiter and Saturn cycles. There is little than can be done to fight them, so the best thing is to work around them, concentrating more on the other areas of your career and simply writing off that cycle. Even if it means shifting careers in midstream, that may be more advisable than going down with a sinking ship. If my jeweler friend had insisted on going the normal buyer route, she would have been out of business in no time. Instead, she became a manufacturer as well as designer, and that new career, along with a particularly favorable Jupiter cycle arriving on time, saved the day.

It is a little difficult to say exactly what the modern career effect of Pluto on a Saturn cycle is but more than likely it will simply serve to make the Saturn cycle more oppressive, so that instead of merely testing an individual, it will have crushing effect. Therefore, when Pluto hits your Saturn cycle, it would be a good idea to sidestep an endeavor entirely if you can figure out a way to do that.

Looking back on your own cycles to date, see where the "wild card" planets fell and observe which cyles they may have upset or suppressed. Then figure on a similar kind of effect the next time you encounter them. They work a bit differently for each person, as do all cycles, so the more self-observation and projection you mix with what's already in this book, the better.

Some additional information may be gleaned from the Tables of Outer Planets and Lunar Nodes giving the positions of these planets. Instead of just giving the general sign position of each, the table gives the degree position within each sign on a yearly basis, since the planets move so slowly. This will enable you to figure out when, for instance, they are likely to be actually on top of your Ascendant, often a very critical time. Since there are 30 degrees in a sign, if your Ascendant falls early in a sign (see note in Ascendant Worksheet), then the "wild card" planets will affect you most when they are in the first 10 degrees of that sign. If your Ascendant falls roughly in the middle of its sign, then the degrees from 10 to 20 will most affect you. If your Ascendant falls late in its sign, then the last 10 degrees will have the most effect.

For example, if your Ascendant fell early in Sagittarius, then the first half of the 1970s, when Neptune was in its first 10 degrees, would have been exceptionally uncertain and changeable with respect to retaining a solid and desirable career position. You might have found a solid but undesirable position, or a desirable but shaky one, but not the best of both.

Similarly, if your Ascendant falls in late Scorpio, then the period from late 1979 through the end of 1981, when Uranus is in the last 10 degrees of that sign, was likely a particularly stormy one, with a lot of sudden and unexpected shakeups in your personality and individual style.

Lastly, as I mentioned before, if you're in for Pluto over your Ascendant, as is about to happen if you have Ascendant in mid-Scorpio, then get ready to really batten down the hatches or gracefully retire for a while. In 1987-91, when Pluto is in the middle 10 degrees of Scorpio, you can expect to get buried. I mean that almost literally—I have never seen

Losing Control

that particular phenomenon in an individual's chart that he or she didn't retire from the scene, either willingly or forcibly, until it was over. It's the single worst career cycle peak there is.

Another thing you may utilize the "wild card" planetary tables for is determining when those planets reach the area of the degree of your natal sun. To find your natal sun degree, just count the days from the beginning of your sun sign until you get to your birthday, and that's it. For example, someone born on March 30 would have the sun around 10° Aries.

The "wild card" planets reaching your natal sun degree usually cause internal personal upheaval and change, which, of course, can have a considerable effect on your career. Therefore, if you see that is about to happen in the near future, do not make definite long-range career commitments, because you may find yourself feeling entirely differently about everything in a little while and regret having boxed yourself in. All this has more basis in traditional astrological lore than in proven cycle research, but I have seen it happen often enough to feel it is worth throwing in.

In the same table as Uranus, Neptune, and Pluto are the positions of the lunar nodes, which have not been discussed so far. They will be dealt with in Chapter 8, so hang on until then.

All the basic career cycles have been described and their effects analyzed. If you're having difficulty pinning down just where and how they work in your own case, the following chapter will describe how they can be put down in simple graph form, just as in high school math and science. Then you'll be able to put your finger on when every cycle hits in your own career and how they interact.

And if math and science were your worst subjects in school (as they were mine), you don't even have to go to the trouble of making up all your own graphs. The most important ones, those of Jupiter and Saturn, are already made up for you at the end of the next chapter!

But you *do* have to learn how to read the graphs, so read the next chapter carefully.

TABLE OF OUTER PLANETS AND LUNAR NODES

January 1 Positions

	Uranus	Neptune	Pluto	North Node	South Node
1920	29AQ	11LE	7CA	22SC	22TA
1921	3PI	13LE	8CA	3SC	3TA
1922	7PI	14LE	9CA	14LI	14AR
1923	10PI	18LE	10CA	24VI	24PI
1924	14PI	20LE	11CA	5VI	5PI
1925	18PI	22LE	13CA	16LE	16AQ
1926	22PI	24LE	14CA	26CA	26CP
1927	26PI	27LE	15CA	7CA	7CP
1928	0AR	29LE	16CA	18GE	18SA
1929	4AR	1VI	17CA	28TA	12SC
1930	8AR	3VI	19CA	9TA	9SC
1931	12AR	6VI	20CA	20AR	20LI
1932	15AR	8VI	21CA	0AR	0LI
1933	19AR	10VI	23CA	11PI	11VI
1934	23AR	12VI	24CA	22AQ	22LE
1935	28AR	15VI	25CA	2AQ	2LE
1936	2TA	17VI	27CA	13CP	13CA
1937	6TA	19VI	28CA	24SA	24GE
1938	10TA	21VI	29CA	4SA	4GE
1939	14TA	23VI	1LE	15SC	15TA
1940	18TA	26VI	2LE	26LI	26AR
1941	23TA	28VI	4LE	6LI	6AR
1942	27TA	0LI	5LE	17VI	17PI
1943	1GE	2LI	7LE	27LE	27AQ
1944	6GE	4LI	8LE	8LE	8AQ
1945	10GE	6LI	10LE	19CA	19CP
1946	14GE	9LI	11LE	29GE	29SA
1947	19GE	11LI	13LE	10GE	10SA
1948	23GE	13LI	14LE	21TA	21SC
1949	28GE	15LI	16LE	1TA	1SC
1950	3CA	17LI	18LE	12AR	12LI
1951	7CA	19LI	20LE	23PI	23VI
1952	12CA	22LI	21LE	4PI	4VI
1953	17CA	24LI	23LE	14AQ	14LE
1954	22CA	26LI	25LE	25CP	25CA
1955	26CA	28LI	27LE	5CP	5CA
1956	1LE	0SC	28LE	16SA	16GE
1957	6LE	2SC	0VI	27SC	27TA
1958	11LE	4SC	2VI	7SC	7TA
1959	16LE	7SC	4VI	18LI	18AR
1960	21LE	9SC	6VI	29VI	29PI
1961	26LE	11SC	8VI	9VI	9PI
1962	0VI	13SC	10VI	20LE	20AQ
1963	5VI	15SC	12VI	1LE	1AQ
1964	10VI	17SC	14VI	11CA	11CP
1965	15VI	19SC	16VI	22GE	22SA
1966	20VI	21SC	19VI	3GE	3SA
1967	25VI	24SC	21VI	13TA	13SC
1968	29VI	26SC	23VI	24AR	24LI
1969	4LI	28SC	25VI	5AR	5LI
1970	9LI	0SA	27VI	15PI	15VI
1971	14LI	2SA	0LI	26AQ	26LE
1972	18LI	4SA	2LI	7AQ	7LE
1973	23LI	6SA	5LI	17CP	17CA

1974	27LI	8SA	7LI	28SA	28GE
1975	2SC	10SA	9LI	9SA	9GE
1976	6SC	13SA	12LI	19SC	19TA
1977	11SC	15SA	14LI	0SC	0TA
1978	15SC	17SA	17LI	11LI	11AR
1979	20SC	19SA	19LI	21VI	21PI
1980	24SC	21SA	22LI	2VI	2PI
1981	29SC	23SA	24LI	13LE	13AQ
1982	3SA	25SA	27LI	23CA	23CP
1983	7SA	27SA	29LI	4CA	4CP
1984	11SA	29SA	2SC	15PI	15VI
1985	16SA	2CP	4SC	25TA	25SC
1986	20SA	4CP	7SC	6TA	6SC
1987	24SA	6CP	10SC	16AR	16LI
1988	28SA	8CP	12SC	25PI	25VI
1989	2CP	11CP	15SC	5PI	5VI
1990	6CP	13CP	17SC	16AQ	16LE
1991	11CP	15CP	20SC	28CP	28CA
1992	15CP	17CP	22SC	10CP	10CA
1993	18CP	19CP	25SC	21SA	21GE
1994	22CP	21CP	27SC	2SA	2GE
1995	26CP	23CP	0SA	12SC	12TA
1996	0AQ	25CP	2SA	21LI	21AR
1997	4AQ	27CP	5SA	1LI	1AR
1998	8AQ	29CP	7SA	11VI	11PI
1999	11AQ	2AQ	9SA	22LE	22AQ
2000	15AQ	4AQ	12SA	3LE	3AQ

AR	— Aries	LE	— Leo	SA	— Sagittarius
TA	— Taurus	VI	— Virgo	CP	— Capricorn
GE	— Gemini	LI	— Libra	AQ	— Aquarius
CA	— Cancer	SC	— Scorpio	PI	— Pisces

7

THE CAREER GRAPH: AN OVERALL ANALYSIS

At this point, with five different long-range planetary cycles to keep track of (excluding the shorter ones like Mars, sun, and moon), things are getting pretty confusing. In order to tell if a given year is going to be good or bad in any one area of life, you have to go paging back and forth between the different tables, trying to juggle everything in your head at the same time.

So now it's time to simplify and put everything covered so far into a simple, concrete form that can be easily analyzed. It's done easily enough by making a graph of the Jupiter and Saturn cycles, and then adding the "wild card" planets on top of them.

Suppose you want to see what the overall picture concerning cash flow and money availability is. That is the No. 2 cycle for both Jupiter and Saturn (and everything else). Using as an example the musician mentioned in the beginning of Chapter 4, here's how it's done:

He has middle to late Gemini Ascendant, so we want to find out when Jupiter and Saturn were in the next sign along, Cancer. Consulting the table, we find Jupiter there in late 1954, 1966, 1978, and so on. These are the Jupiter cycle peaks, and where they go to later dates than are covered by the tables, we merely keep adding 12 years to get the positions. Where they are included in the span of the tables, it is important to use the listed positions, as the cycle varies a bit every now and then and isn't always exactly 12 years.

To obtain the cycle bottoms, we take the Jupiter positions the seventh sign from Cancer, in middle to late Capricorn. These we find in 1961, late 1972, and so on. We connect the positions, and we then have a graph of No. 2 Jupiter cycle highs and lows for the entire lifetime (assuming he doesn't survive past age 84).

Then we do the same thing with Saturn positions, finding that Saturn was in middle to late Cancer in 1945 (at birth), late 1974, and so on. Then we look up when Saturn was passing through middle to late Capricorn, and mark down the year. Again,

CONSTRUCTING THE CAREER CYCLE GRAPH

Suppose, for instance, you were born in 1945 and had early Aries Ascendant and wanted to set up a No. 1 cycle chart. You would look up each time Jupiter came into early Aries and mark it at the top of the chart. Then you would look up each time Jupiter came into the opposite sign, Libra, and mark that at the bottom of the chart. Then connect the marks, top and bottom, in chronological order to create the even Jupiter cycle (dotted line).

Do the same thing for Saturn, marking when it came into early Aries (top) and early Libra (bottom) and then connecting the marks in chronological order (solid line). There you have your completed No. 1 cycle chart. It comes out even clearer if you use different-colored pens—say, red for Jupiter and blue for Saturn.

Here you can clearly see a difficult period beginning around age 19 when the Jupiter and Saturn lines cross, peaking at age 22 when Saturn is in Aries. Ages 27 to 44 look pretty good with nothing but Jupiter peaks (in Aries) at age 30 and a Saturn bottom (in Libra). Then another difficult period that peaks at age 51 (Saturn in Aries), giving way to an excellent period focusing on the Jupiter peak (in Aries) at age 66—the nicest period since the Jupiter peak and Saturn low at age 6 or 7.

This is, of course, only a No. 1 cycle chart. If you wanted to do a No. 5 cycle, for instance, you would use the entry of Jupiter and Saturn into the fifth sign away (Leo) for peaks and its opposite (Aquarius) for bottoms. See chart page 108.

---

where dates go outside the span of the tables, just add 29½ years (the Saturn cycle) to get your next position.

Now we have a graph that looks like Chart A, depicting the Jupiter and Saturn ups and downs in relation to the No. 2, or monetary, cycle. In this form, not only can we see the individual movements on an overall scale, but we can see their dynamic relation to one another as well, which is very important. Together, they paint a picture of the availability of funds in this person's life on a year-to-year basis. Here is how to read the description:

We see a first Jupiter and a Saturn low at age 15 and 16, respectively. This is not too meaningful, as he was still living at home and income was not a source of concern. To discover his economic conditions then, we would have to examine the same graph for the breadwinner in his family. But where the Jupiter cycle going up crosses the Saturn cycle going down (circled), a real decision of financial import was made—he decided to become a professional musician. His field was folk music, and that doesn't offer much of a career these days, but in the sixties all things were thought possible. After all, Peter, Paul, and Mary were raking in a bundle at the time.

Actually, the decision wasn't half bad as far as money was concerned, even though it caused him to skip college in favor of an immediate career in music. After a few years he found himself in pop music with a fat contract at a large record company and toured the country with a rock group. By age 21, where the Jupiter cycle peaks, he had enough money to start his own recording company, and his innovative ideas attracted considerable outside investment.

As I previously mentioned, however, he did not keep his eye on the ball, and as investors crowded in, his company got cut into finer and finer pieces, significantly reducing his share and function in it along the way. By almost age 24, when the Saturn

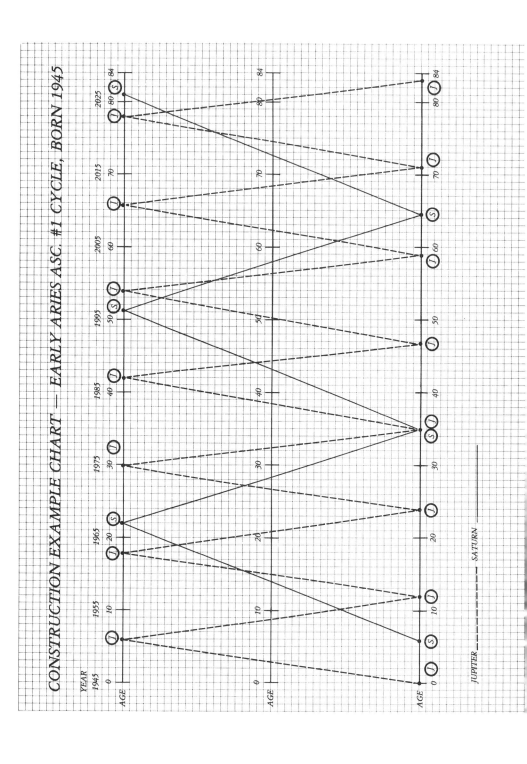

CONSTRUCTION EXAMPLE CHART — EARLY ARIES ASC. #1 CYCLE, BORN 1945

JUPITER _____   SATURN _____

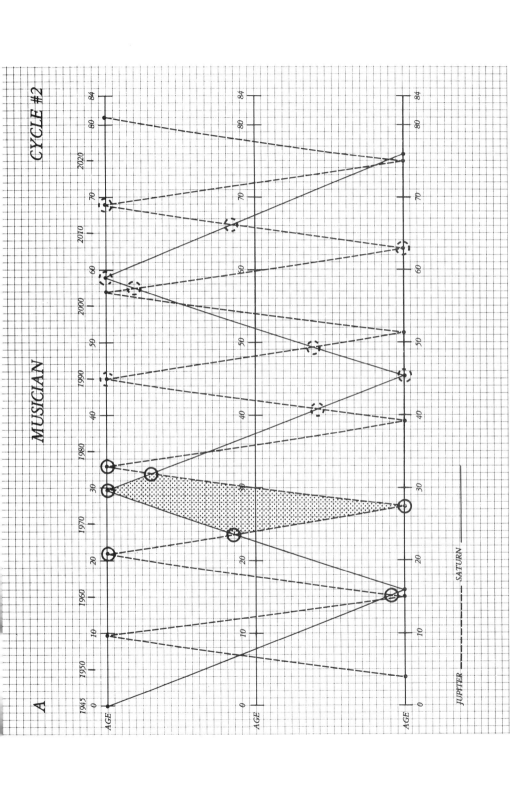

and Jupiter cycles again crossed, he found that he had lost control of the whole thing and within a year was out on the street with practically nothing. The Saturn cycle (going up) and the Jupiter cycle (going down) had exchanged influences and there would be many hard times to come.

He tried to stay in the field, using his talents as a songwriter (more about that later) to keep him going. But eventually that dried up on him and in order to make ends meet, he took a job as an assistant editor on a national magazine. In this entirely new career, he worked his way up from the bottom, and his writing efforts eventually culminated in the publication of several books (when Jupiter going up again crossed Saturn going down). He finally reached relative financial stability again when Jupiter hit its cycle peak.

That is where matters stand for him as of this writing. The Jupiter and Saturn cycles clearly outlined his cash situation over his entire career. The peaks represented considerable wealth (at 21) with Jupiter and abject poverty (at 29) with Saturn, and the critical turning points that brought both were marked when the two cycles crossed (at 15 and 32).

If he had been aware of this graph in the sixties, when the critical events were occurring, he might have been more careful in his moves and perhaps would not have suffered such extremities. Certainly he could have done nothing to prevent the Saturn-dominated period from occurring, short of sending an expedition to blow up the planet, but perhaps he could have softened its blow by paying closer attention to where his money was coming from.

Certainly he will keep an eye on it in the future, which looks as if it has much better things in store for him. Both Jupiter and Saturn cycles are declining now, so they will essentially cancel each other out and his situation should remain stable until age 41, at which time some important break should occur as Jupiter (going up) crosses Saturn (going down), ushering in a period of considerable wealth. This focuses around 45 (Jupiter peak) and 46 (Saturn bottom) and he will do well to do everything possible to preserve funds acquired then so the difficulties beginning at age 49 (another crossing point) won't take too heavy a toll. Actually, they probably won't as both Jupiter and Saturn quickly rise together a couple of years later, indicating regained stability. Indeed, looking at the rest of the chart, it is clear that he will never again experience such a drastic shortage of funds as occurred in the period marked off by the Saturn peak and Jupiter low (shaded area).

Perhaps. But we still haven't looked at the "wild card" planets to see if they might significantly dampen the period of bounty for this person in his mid-40s. When we include them, the graph looks like Chart B. Here we see that instead of peaking during that period and suppressing it, they in fact safely bottom out, so the Jupiter period should proceed as forecast.

SPECIAL NOTE:

In some cases, neither a peak nor a bottom will occur for one or more of the "wild card" planets during the lifetime being considered because of the great length of these planetary cycles. In that case, a mid-cycle point of four signs ahead or behind the cycle sign being considered can be placed on the middle line of the graph, and a rough approxi-

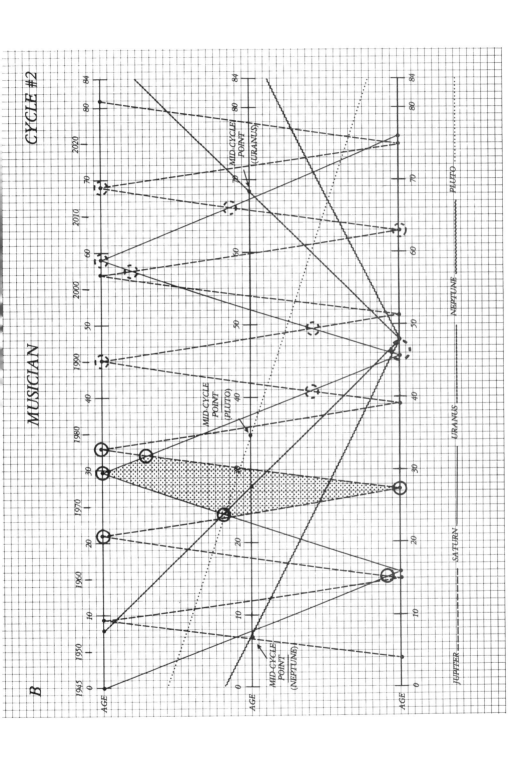

B   MUSICIAN   CYCLE #2

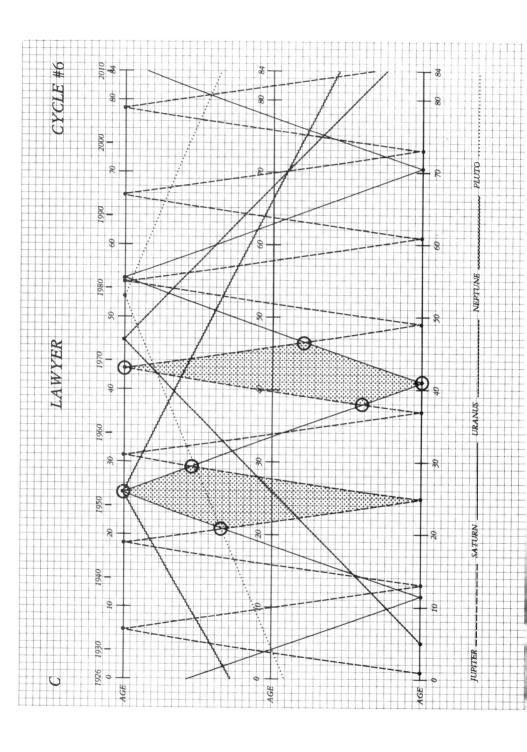

C   1926 1930   LAWYER   CYCLE #6

JUPITER ———— SATURN ———— URANUS ———— NEPTUNE ———— PLUTO ············

mate cycle line drawn through it (as with Pluto on this one, which is marked in mid to late Libra here as its mid-cycle point). Actually, in such a case, you might as well leave it out, as it only serves to make another confusing line on the graph and basically has no effect on the cycle concerned. For simplicity's sake, this approach may be taken with all three "wild card"planets, marking just their cycle peaks where they might interfere with Jupiter and Saturn with a short, 4- or 5-year-long bar on the graph. However, I like to draw the full graph anyway because I believe crossing points between Jupiter and Saturn and these planets may intensify certain crucial areas (as Pluto did in the musician's case at age 24, when he was "muscled" out of the corporation).

Let us take another example where the "wild card" planets really do make things worse at an already bad time. In this instance, it is the case of the woman I mentioned in the last chapter who found herself relegated to the position of girl Friday despite her law degree. Here we have the chart (Chart C) of her combined sixth cycle, having to do with the ability to get essentially busywork projects done with a maximum demonstration of talent and professional skill.

It can be seen that at age 21, when she decided to go to law school the following year, things were already headed down hill in this respect. Not suspecting that her decision was critical in a negative sense, being right at the crossing of Jupiter (going down) and Saturn (going up), she ploughed ahead and made it through law school. The decision was a particularly compulsive one, because she wasn't all that interested in the law, but looked upon it as a way of proving to the world that she could do anything she chose, possibly indicated by the intersection of the Pluto line with the Saturn and Jupiter.

Right at the peak of the Saturn cycle, Neptune also peaked, and with Jupiter at its low, the whole combination served to trap her in a situation she could neither cope with nor gracefully get out of, beginning at age 26, when she graduated from law school, and ending at age 29, when she finally gave up, another compulsive and rather sudden decision marked by the Pluto intersection.

At least, however, Jupiter was on its way up, so she experienced a certain elation and freedom from the drudgery she had been subjected to. But that was only temporary and Jupiter and Saturn ran more or less together until age 37, when a declining Saturn crossed a rising Jupiter and started one of the busiest and most positive periods in her life—she became heavily involved with both the women's movement and consumer advocacy (she was one of Nader's Raiders). Back in the legal profession at last, she again was overwhelmed with busywork, but it was in an area of real interest and concern to her, and she was receiving a great deal of respect and praise for her efforts. Finally, when Jupiter and Saturn again crossed, with Uranus making its peak cycle about the same time, she inherited a large sum of money from her father's estate and was suddenly able to start her own firm at age 47. Since then, her work load has stayed on a fairly even keel, after a brief difficult period of getting established on her own, as after age 49 Jupiter and Saturn began running pretty much together.

What could she have done to alter her career if she had had this graph at her disposal from the beginning? Well, either she could have picked an easier way of launching herself in the legal profession, or she could have chosen a profession with less busywork and discrimination and thus have avoided the whole issue. But in the latter case, she wouldn't have wound up as a successful lawyer, though perhaps she would

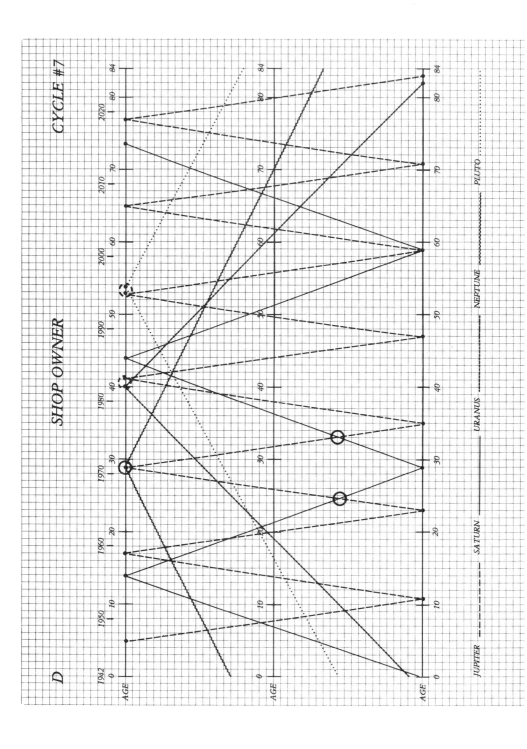

D SHOP OWNER CYCLE #7

JUPITER --------- SATURN _____ URANUS _____ NEPTUNE ~~~~~~~~ PLUTO ....

have been just as successful in whatever other field she chose. In either case, she would have been better informed about what she was facing and might have been able to make a more educated decision one way or another.

Let's take another case where a "wild card" interfered with the Jupiter-Saturn relationship, this time spoiling what should have been a very positive seventh cycle. Here we have a graph (Chart D) of the seventh cycle of the head-shop owner I mentioned in the last chapter. The Jupiter peak at age 29, along with its concomitant Saturn low, should have brought him lots of good partners who would work out well. Unfortunately, Neptune was at its peak also, and the partners who did come flocking in turned out to be deceitful and ran him right out of his own business. In this case, the crossover points on either side of this period at ages 24 and 33 (circled) don't describe the length of life of the business, but merely of his inclination to get involved with other people in general.

Moreover, it is doubtful if he will gain very much by the experience, as the two succeeding Jupiter peaks coincide with Uranus and Pluto peaks, which will bring him more ill from any alliances he makes then. It would therefore seem better for him to avoid partnerships entirely and rely mainly on himself. In fact, this graph may keep him from getting hurt by people he thinks are his allies and therefore prevent a very sour outlook on personal relationships in the future.

Personal style can have a lot to do with the way cycle charts should be interpreted. Some people get depressed during Jupiter lows, for instance, while others see them as a challenge to be seized and turned to advantage. One such person was publisher Bob Harrison, whose checkered career led him in and out of the public limelight for forty years.

Harrison originated the format of the "girlie" magazine back in the forties, and later started the greatest scandal sheet of them all, *Confidential* magazine, which probably ruined more careers than any publication in history and which at its prime was the widest selling magazine in the world. But all these, as well as his later efforts, were much more than money to him—they were vehicles for his personality and kept him in front of the public, in whose recognition and adulation he loved to bask. He was a very charming and sociable man, and his favorite hobby was hanging out with the Beautiful People of the period and feeling very much admired and envied (sometimes even hated) by the world at large.

Thus, when we look at a No. 1 cycle chart (Chart E), describing cycles of pure personality, we find that every time there was a Jupiter low and the world was beginning to ignore or tire of him, he would start some new project to get people looking his way again. The first really successful projects, started in the early 1940s, were the girlie magazines, with titles like *Beauty Parade*, *Wink*, and *Eyeful*. They were the first magazines to combine pinups with an editorial theme, and the same format is still with us in magazines like *Playboy*, *Penthouse*, and *Hustler*. Harrison mixed in a number of fetishes, such as black fishnet stockings, whips and chains, and other offbeat accoutrements and gained a reputation as a daring young shocker in the publishing trade.

In the late forties these magazines, started on the No. 1 Jupiter low, were quite successful, but by the early fifties they were just another product on the magazine rack and Harrison was no longer a household word. So, during that period of personal

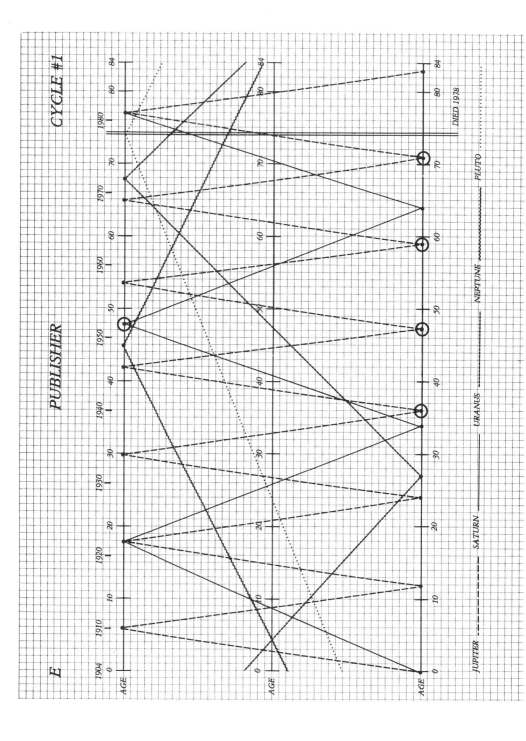

PUBLISHER   CYCLE #1

JUPITER ------   SATURN -------   URANUS ———   NEPTUNE ———   PLUTO ·········

DIED 1978

eclipse, at a No. 1 Saturn high and Jupiter low, he began his biggest project of all, *Confidential* magazine.

After a few short years of hard work *Confidential* made him a multimillionaire, and he spent his nights and weekends hobnobbing with Hollywood's finest or jet-setting around the world. At the height of his financial success, however, he was forced to sell the magazine or face a criminal libel suit in California where the attorney general was determined to put him behind bars for the well-documented scandal stories the magazine specialized in. Essentially, he was railroaded out of the business.

Eclipsed before the public, though loaded with dough, he used his following Jupiter low to start another project, a sensationalist tabloid weekly called the *Inside News*, begun in 1963. In the mid-1960s he was back in the public eye again, and even had a forty-page chapter devoted to him in one of the writer Tom Wolfe's best-sellers.

But before long the blood-and-sex tabloid formula became passe, and the most successful of these magazines, *The National Enquirer*, turned into a housewife's weekly, leaving stragglers like *Inside News* to die slowly on the sidelines. Eclipsed again, and now past 70, Harrison refused to give up and retire with his wealth, as most people would have done. Instead, at his Jupiter low, he began work on a publishing imprint that would launch him into that part of the publishing industry.

With a rapidly rising Jupiter cycle in play, the chances are he would have succeeded again, but this time another cycle intervened to prevent it. Pluto's No. 1 cycle peaked in early 1978 and Harrison died of a massive coronary, with Pluto sitting on the exact degree of his Ascendant. He had met the final eclipse. Had he been a younger man he probably would have used that most difficult cycle of all to make an even bigger success, but because of his age and a generally weakened condition, his health was just not up to it.

Harrison's story illustrated that the relative importance of the different cycle graphs to a career depends to a large extent on the individual's personal style and ambitions. Another important factor is the nature of the career. If it is primarily concerned with money-making or money handling (e.g., banking or accounting), the No. 2 or No. 8 cycle will be of particular importance, along with perhaps the No. 6. If, on the other hand, the career depends on spontaneity and creativity, the No. 5 cycle will be of critical importance. Using the example of our unwise musician friend again, we can see how that works. In his No. 5 cycle (Chart F), the creative potential is mapped out clearly in terms of time, beginning with his first songwriting efforts at around age 20, when Jupiter on its way up crosses Saturn on its way down. The peak is in 1969, when he found himself out of the company he started and depending on songwriting for a living. During the whole period he wrote about 150 songs, mostly in the year of the peak and the following year.

At age 28, however, the songs ceased to come—the muse clammed up and that was it. He wrote his last song in that year, and hasn't written one since. As a result, his source of income dried up and he was again forced to find another way to make a living. It's just as well that he did, because he won't have another comparably creative period until the 1990s, and that's a long time to go without eating.

Would awareness of the cycle graph have helped him? It wouldn't have prolonged his productive period as a songwriter, but it would have enabled him to prepare himself for another career. This would have made his career transition a little easier.

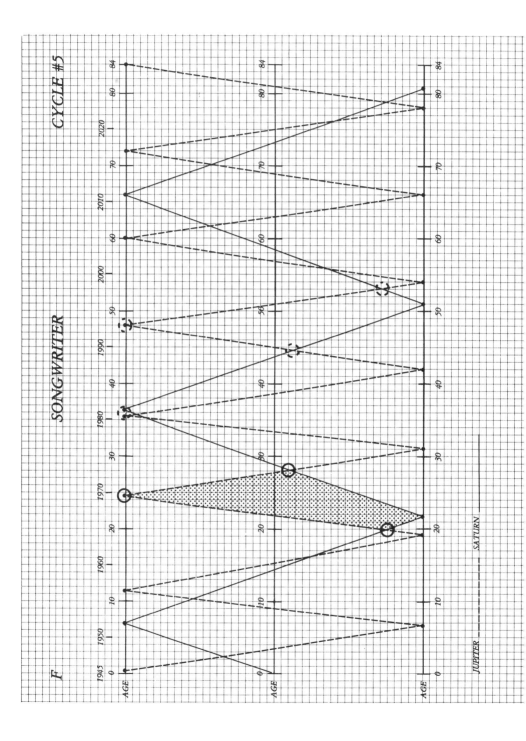

Quite off the topic of career, this No. 5 cycle, as I mentioned before, is also sometimes associated with degree and variety of sexual activity. The same years in this person's life (age 20-28) were a period of maximum activity in that area, during which he had all the perquisites of a pop music figure, including sexual variety. At the end of the period he married and settled down to a much more monogamous, if still enjoyable, sexual life.

Career cycles apply to big and small, success and failure alike, and no better example can be found than in three of the major figures surrounding the Watergate scandal that rocked so many careers, turning unknowns into rising stars and ruining the careers of the most powerful.

In a long-term sense, reputation is the touchstone of politics, so it would certainly be the No. 10 cycle that would be the most important in determining likely ups and downs. Thus, we turn to Richard Nixon's No. 10 cycle, Chart G. Since there were no significant "wild card" cycles here for No. 10, I have left them out, as I did for the previous No. 5 cycle.

What results is a startlingly clear picture of Nixon's career. He began his political career in the late 1940s, but his first claim to national fame was the Alger Hiss case in 1950, which landed him a Senate seat. That was the year Jupiter (going up) crossed Saturn (going down). At the Jupiter peak, in 1953, he was sworn in as Vice President of the United States.

His losing race against John F. Kennedy is marked by the Jupiter low, with Saturn rising. During the middle sixties Saturn and Jupiter were moving along together, maintaining the status quo, and to top it off, Pluto was passing directly over Nixon's middle Virgo Ascendant, putting him into total eclipse. We quite literally didn't have Nixon to kick around anymore.

But he bounced back from this heavy Pluto cycle and after a nice Jupiter peak managed to get himself elected President—but at a very odd time, when Saturn (rising) intersected Jupiter (descending) in 1968. Therefore getting elected President in 1968 should prove the beginning of a very negative period in his career. Indeed, being President and trying too hard to stay there were to be his downfall.

Between the time Jupiter bottomed out and Saturn reached its peak is the critical period—Watergate. Within a year of the Saturn peak he was out of office and in disgraced exile in California. The period finally ended in 1976, with the next Jupiter-Saturn exchange, the year he finally would have left office but for Watergate. Thus we see that despite all appearances to the contrary, getting elected President at the critical turnover point entering a negative cycle was the worst thing that could have happened to Nixon and turned out to be his ruin.

This sounds awfully fatalistic, painting the picture of a political giant dashed to the ground by the ineluctable motions of the planets. Actually, it's not. Nixon was simply going into office with a lot working against him, and under that kind of cycle influence, he needed to be especially careful to guard against things that would spoil is reputation. Instead, he was sloppy and foolish in just those areas, and it spelled the end for him. Other Presidents before him had been equally careless in the same areas, but they didn't have the planetary factors working against them that Nixon did.

But with this negative cycle at its peak in 1972-1973, how did he manage to get elected to his second term? Why wasn't his reputation already bad enough to cause

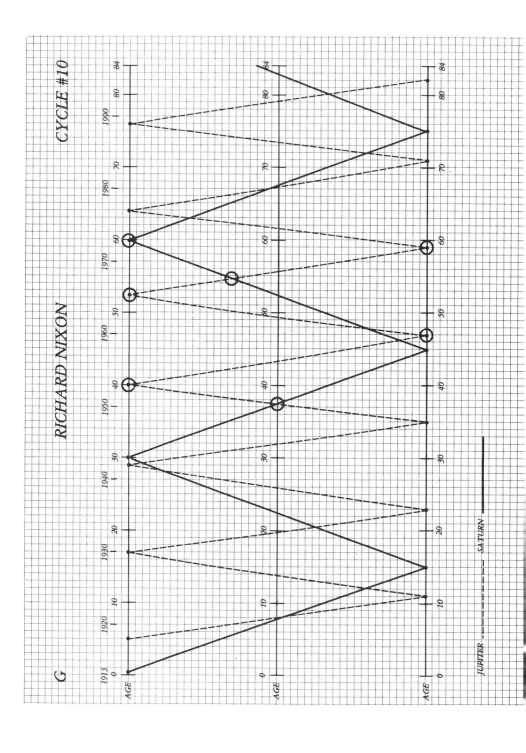

RICHARD NIXON   CYCLE #10

JUPITER · · · · · · · · · · · SATURN _____

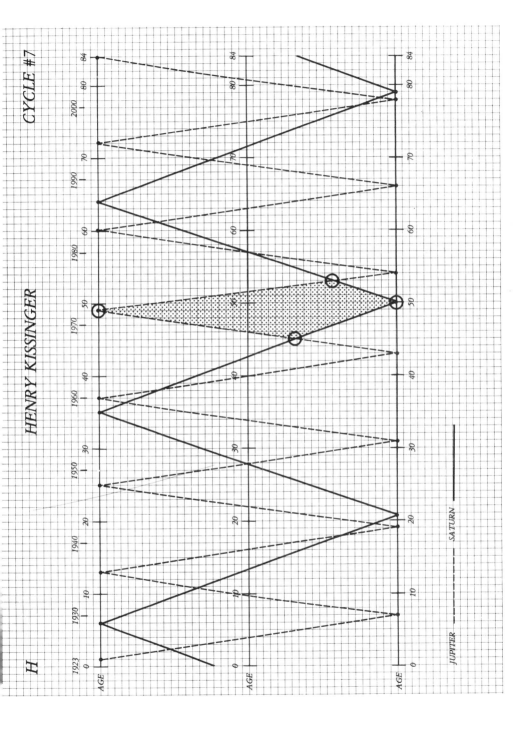

CYCLE #7

HENRY KISSINGER

H

JUPITER --------- SATURN ————

defeat at the polls? The answer to that lies in the cycle analysis of two other figures critical to the election: Henry Kissinger and George McGovern.

Kissinger was employed by Nixon primarily as a negotiator, so his No. 7 cycle of partner dealings would indicate his success in those endeavors. Here (Chart H) we find his association with the Nixon administration clearly mapped out. He joined it at the beginning in 1968, when Jupiter (rising) crossed Saturn (descending) and the Jupiter peak and Saturn bottom coincided exactly with his successful negotiations ending America's involvement in the Vietnam war. It was these peace talks, and the virtual certainty that they could only be concluded successfully if the same team were kept in office, that were the main issue in the election. Otherwise, the outcome of the vote would have been more uncertain. Add to that the effects of Watergate and the dirty tricks campaign (yet to come to light at the election), and the vote was assured—though, in essence, it was Kissinger who was elected, not Nixon.

The other factor that sealed the Democrats' fate and got Nixon into office despite himself and the negative cycle he was going through was George McGovern. Like Kissinger, his Ascendant is in Gemini, but negotiation wasn't what he was up to that year—his business as challenger to the incumbent President was confrontation. He wasn't running on his record and reputation, but rather on what he personally proposed to do to change the situation. Thus what we look at is the No. 1 cycle to see how strong he was at the time in the confrontation game.

A single look at the graph (Chart I) tells the story. During the election of 1972 McGovern was at an all-time cycle low in this area, with Jupiter bottoming out and Saturn peaking. It was a period of particular cycle stress, and not a time to rush into strenuous national confrontations. It is clear from this that the Democrats picked the wrong man to run—almost anyone else would have been a stronger candidate, though not necessarily a better President once elected.

When we use this cycle analysis technique, new light is thrown on the whole confused, turbulent period of Watergate. At the same time, a principle of much more importance to most people personally is illustrated. This chapter demonstrates the importance of being aware not only of one's own cycle situation at any given time, but of others' cycle standings as well. Had the Democrats known this, they might have picked someone else to run, someone not as afflicted by cycle difficulties as McGovern. So, too, the same principles may be applied in everyday business dealings, particularly in deciding whom to use for what purposes. A person undergoing a strong No. 1 cycle Jupiter peak and Saturn low would be an ideal pick for a dynamic sales representative, while someone with a strong No. 2 Jupiter peak would be a more likely investor, having more money to play around with and the inclination to use it. On the other hand, hiring an art director for a project with a peaking Saturn No. 5 cycle could get you only the dullest and most uncreative results.

This is not to say that people undergoing difficult career cycles should be blackballed until they're over. Rather, you should take these matters into consideration so that you don't pick the wrong person for the job, or load him down with more work than he can handle or work that doesn't suit his capabilities. The same goes for you. Try to skirt areas of stress, because they will be harder to deal with and you will get less profit for more work from them. Try to pick areas of endeavor that your current high cycles will favor and give you an extra boost. Wait until difficult cycles are over before

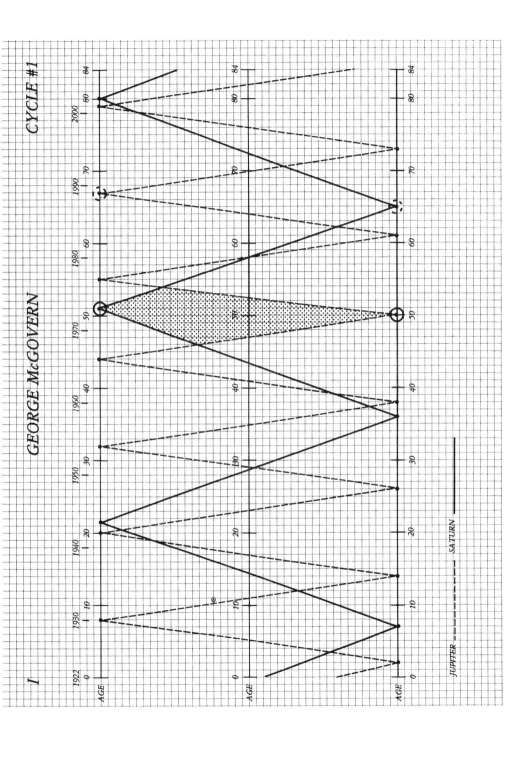

GEORGE McGOVERN   CYCLE #1

you put the full weight of career dependence on those particular areas. You can still learn from them during difficult periods, but you should try to avoid relying on a given area to produce your income when that is under planetary stress. Thus, if you understand your patterns of planetary interaction through each of the twelve cycles, you will know just when and where your strong and weak points will occur. This awareness will give you a decided advantage, because you will know well ahead of time what trends are in the making, and will be able to make adjustments and focus your attention accordingly, with greater speed and accuracy than might otherwise be the case.

In order to make sure you've got your cycles drawn up correctly, review where they have already fallen in your life and see how and when they affected you. If, when you check your cycles next to pertinent events of your past you find that a cycle is off by a year or so (which may happen for reasons mentioned earlier), you may correct it so that the occurence of cycle and event becomes consistent. However, it would be wise to regard your correction as tentative, checking and rechecking events as they happen, until you feel you have arrived at your true cycle layout. That way you'll be sure your future anticipations are correct and you won't find something catching you by surprise early or have to wait an extra year for something you're expecting to happen.

The best way to get an accurate view of your cycles is to draw them up yourself—but if you've already tried making one up, you can see that drawing all twelve could be more than a little time-consuming. If you're willing to sacrifice some degree of exactitude, however, you can read all twelve of your Jupiter and Saturn cycles in the twelve graphs that follow. These are made up for the middle of each sign, and all you have to do is match the sign to your cycle number and you're ready to go. If your Ascendant falls roughly in the middle of a sign to begin with, they're all exact for you as they stand. If your Ascendant is early in its sign, they'll run a trifle late (up to a year) and if your Ascendant falls late in its sign, they'll run a trifle early by the same amount. To get an even more complete picture, you can xerox them and draw in the "wild card" planet lines—all in all, a much quicker and easier process than drawing everything up from scratch.

ANOTHER USEFUL TOOL:

You will note that the following graphs have horizontal lines running through them labelled ½, ⅓, and ⅙. These mark what astrologers would call harmonic or aspect divisions of the planetary cycles and they will give you a further clue about the nature of coming events. If a Jupiter-Saturn crossover occurs on or near a ⅓ or ⅙ line, then the transition from one trend to the next will be relatively easy and marked more by outside events acting upon you rather than willful achievements of your own. An example is Nixon's #10 cycle crossover in 1968 which was on the ⅓ line—he was swept into power by others' mistakes. On the same graph, however, the crossover in 1950 was on the ½ line, meaning the transition was made through struggle and effort and although beneficial, may not have seemed a pleasant way to go about it at the time. This is generally a safe rule to follow: ⅓ and ⅙ mean easy transition keyed to external forces, ½ indicates struggle and testing in which you will have to make the changes happen yourself, often against the odds.

AND ONE FINAL NOTE (FOR ASTROLOGERS):

If you are already an astrologer (or studying to become one), you will have noticed by this time that this book is a description of transit cycles to the twelve houses of the nativity, based on the equal house system erected from the Ascendant. Don't like the equal house system?—Insert your own house cusps and erect the graphs from there: Placidus, Koch, Campanus, Regiomontanus, topocentric, what have you. Since the system is based on long-range mean cycles, the difference in accuracy won't be much for the inner houses, but for the MC and IC it could make a difference of a year or two. Have fun . . . the astrological implications of this technique are enormous (for instance, those crossover points describe *transiting* midpoints of the bodies in question over the house cusp concerned) . . . .

ARIES

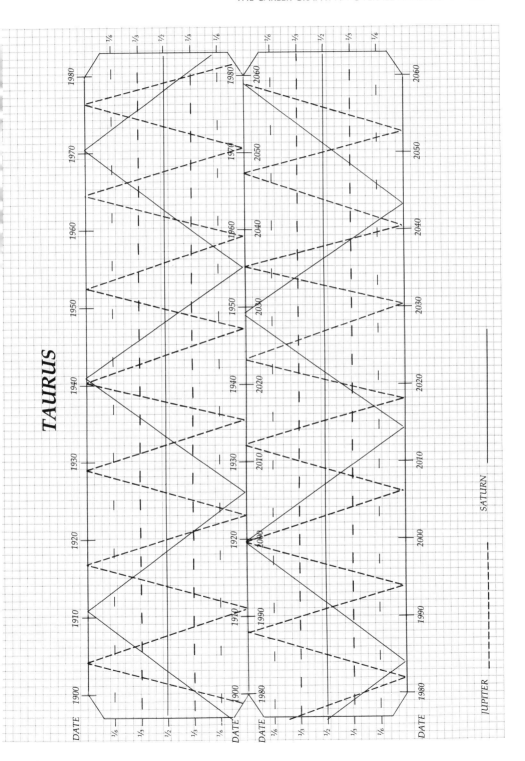

TAURUS

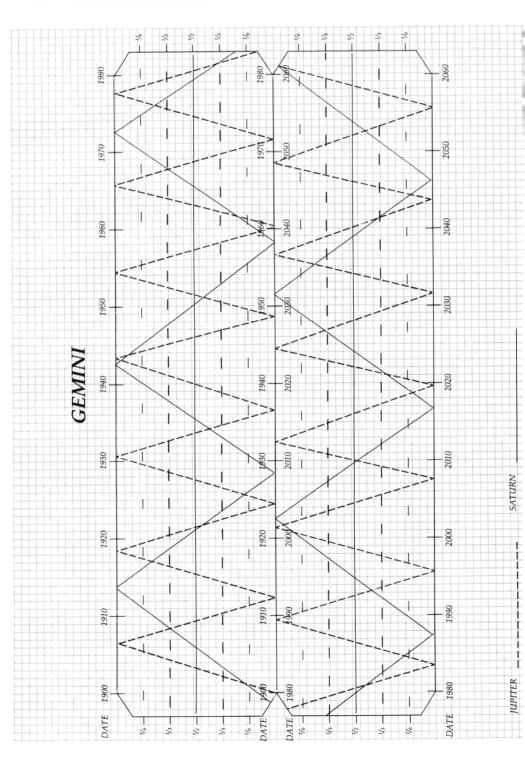

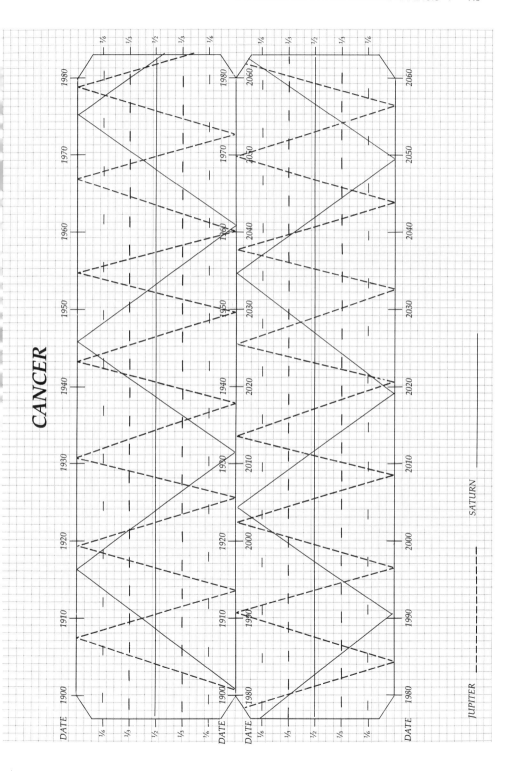

CANCER

LEO

DATE

SATURN

JUPITER

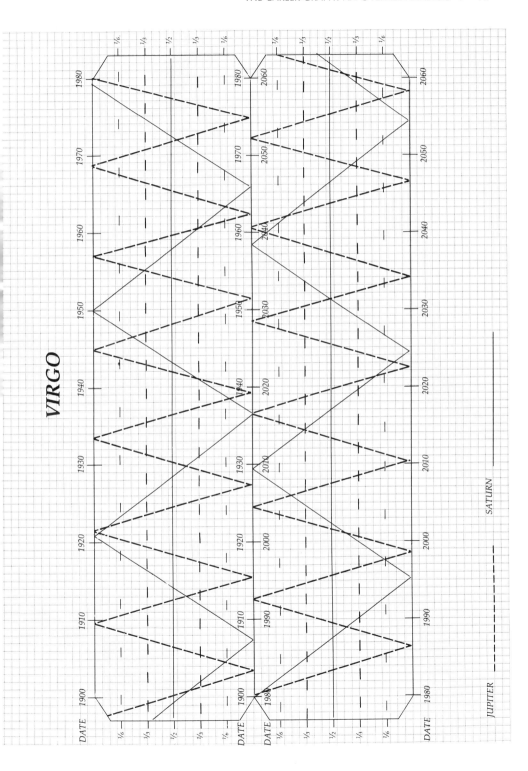

VIRGO

SATURN ——————

JUPITER - - - - - -

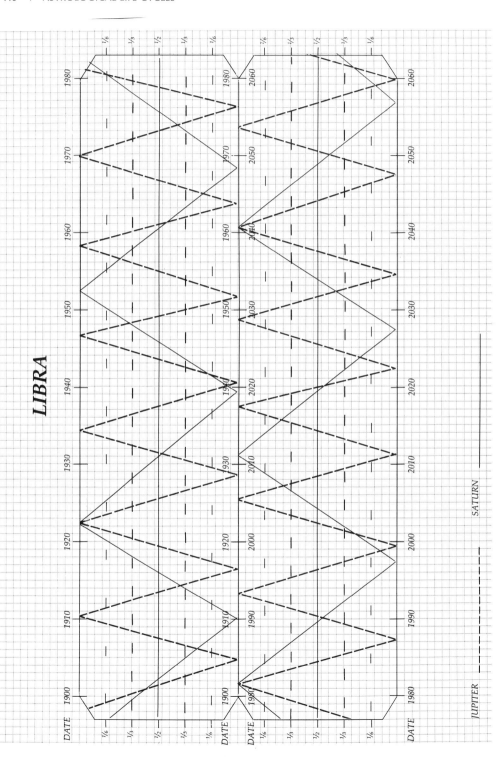

LIBRA

SATURN

JUPITER

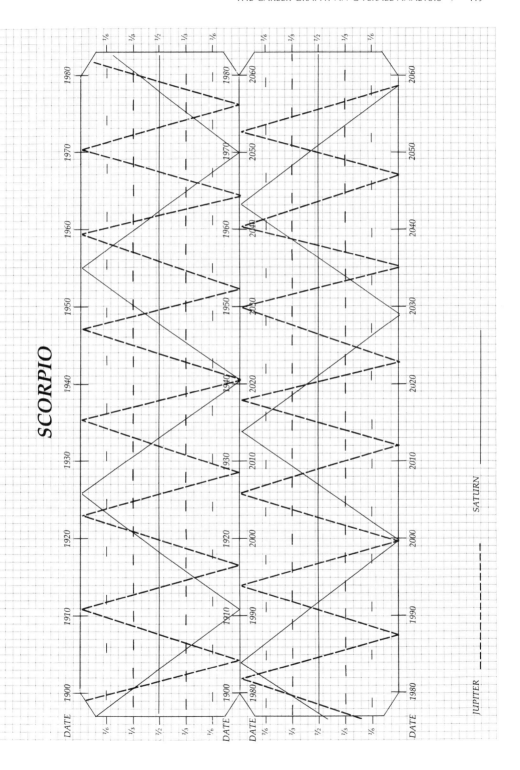

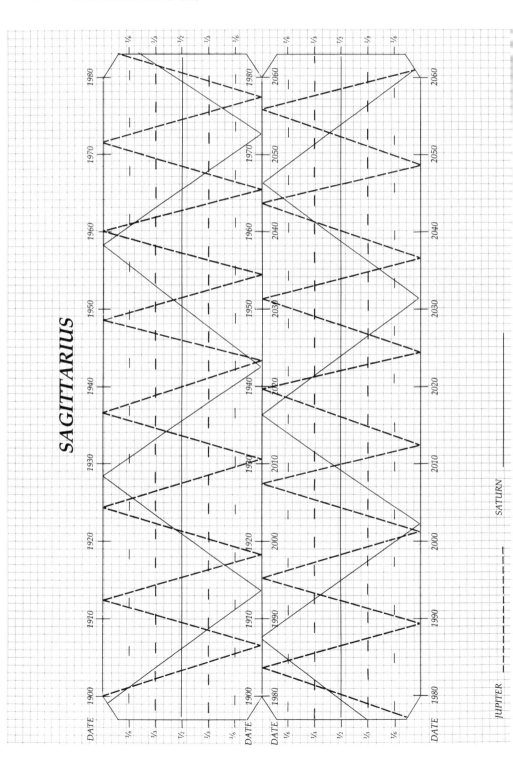

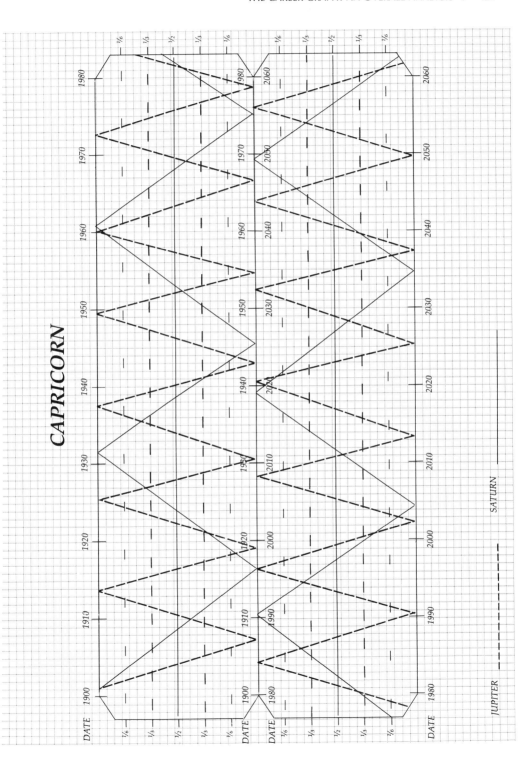

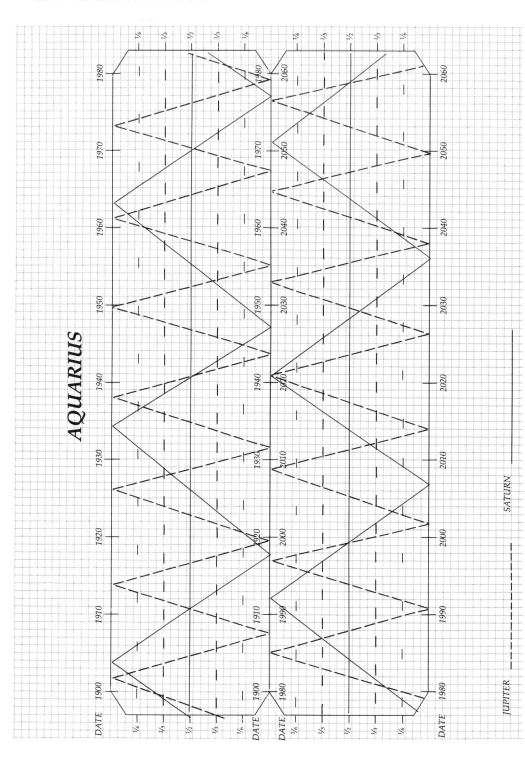

AQUARIUS

SATURN

JUPITER

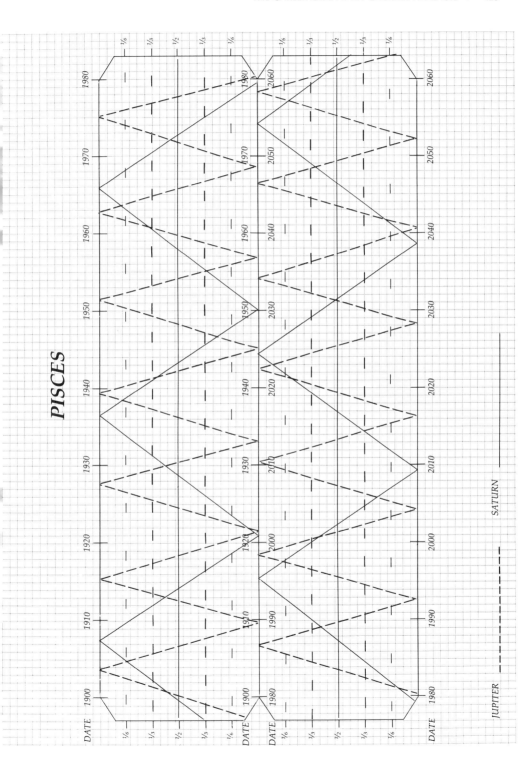

PISCES

8

FRIENDS AND ENEMIES:
HOW TO TELL THE DIFFERENCE

In planning your overall career strategy and your day-to-day on-the-job tactics, it is obviously essential to know who your friends and enemies are—who is going to give you a boost and who is looking to shoot down your efforts at success. It is surprising how little we often know about who can help us and who might hurt us. So often the friend we thought would put in a good word for us with the boss winds up making a play for the very position we were looking for—showing his true colors too late for us to do anything about it. And not infrequently our toughest competitor turns into a sudden ally when a third threatening party enters the race.

In the end you have to rely on your common sense and good judgment, taking all possible factors into account when deciding who is on your side and how long he is likely to remain there. But certain shared positions within planetary cycles can add a new dimension to your understanding and serve as clues to how your colleagues will relate to you.

In traditional astrology this chart comparison is called "synastry," and it consists of matching the natal planetary positions of two individuals to see if similar areas of the birth chart are occupied. Where the same spot is occupied by two planets of conflicting natures in either chart, then astrological tradition postulates that the two individuals will tend to harm each other. Where the planetary natures blend well, then they will tend to help each other out.

This analysis is just tradition, with nothing concrete to back it up, but it has tested out excellently so there would appear to be something to it. For instance, in the controversial Joann Little case, where Little was accused of murdering the jailer who tried to rape her, the defense used comparative astrology to choose jurors. The defense asked prospective jurors their birth dates, and in cases where potentially damaging planets (such as Saturn, Uranus, Neptune, Pluto, and Mars) shared degree areas with Little's own birth chart, the jurors were excused. Where supposedly "benefic" planets (Venus, sun, Jupiter) shared those areas, then the defense okayed the jurors. As is widely known, the defendant was acquitted.

One example doesn't "prove" an astrological premise—perhaps any combination of jurors would have acquitted her. But there are other instances of precisely such applications of astrology. I myself have used the same technique repeatedly in civil cases to help clients choose juries, and have never lost a case. In fact, in one case it was even possible to predict who would be chosen jury foreman by this method. I also know of others who have used the same technique successfully, so perhaps there is something to it.

It is possible to find a quite logical model with which to explain this phenomenon. First, we know from Gauquelin's research that natal planetary positions in relation to the Ascendant point are statistical indicators of career occupations. Second, we found that the cycles of the planets in relation to their natal positions clearly outline the accepted psychological life-crisis periods. Combining these two principles, we theorized that planetary cycles focusing on the career-influencing Ascendant might relate to overall career cycles, and then found that to be the case.

Now, going one step further, we may surmise that a planetary cycle may have observable effects not only when focused on the Ascendant or its own natal position but also when focused on natal positions of other planets as well. Such cycles, if successfully tested, would go a long way in explaining and describing the effects alleged by astrologers.

It would also explain the observed "synastry" effect that has been seen and used in the courts. I have often witnessed that same effect operating in career situations, often to the great detriment of people who might have avoided trouble if they had been aware of it. Simply, if one person's natal Jupiter position is, say, 15° Virgo and another's natal Saturn position is also 15° Virgo, then they will both be receiving synchronous cycle peaks to those planets from all the regular celestial cycles, from the shorter diurnal and lunar cycles all the way to the very longest cycles of many years. However, when one individual is receiving a "positive" boost to expansive Jupiter, the other will be getting a "negative" boost to restrictive Saturn. This comparison will help to pinpoint the time when negative influences run high in one individual synchronous with positive influences in the other, creating a general life rhythm in which the Saturn individual has a negative effect on the Jupiter individual, and the Jupiter individual has a positive effect on the Saturn individual. The effect is similar to putting a sad person and a happy person in the same room—the sad person will get somewhat cheerier, and the happy one will tend to get more depressed.

One would obviously prefer to be the person receiving the cheering, positive effects. That, in a nutshell, is the art of career self-defense—at least as far as planetary factors are concerned. If you know what the different combinations of planets between your own nativity and that of another signify, you will have some idea of the positive or negative influence that person may have on your career efforts.

How does one know how to interpret these different crossover contacts? Well, the rest of this chapter is a compendium of the meanings of the different crossovers, compiled from my own personal observations over the years, and supplemented by traditional astrological lore. I cannot guarantee it 100 percent because there hasn't been any clinical research yet—and it may be a long time coming, because clinically defining "friend" and "enemy" is a pretty foggy business. But I think you will find that it is on target surprisingly often, so you would do well to heed it.

Included, along with the sun and the other planets, are the lunar nodes, the moving points in space where the orbit of the moon intersects the orbit of the earth. Although not actual bodies in themselves, they are the critical linking points in space between earth, sun, and moon, and determine the eclipse cycle, so they are well worth taking note of as sensitive points.

Finding Your Contact Points

First of all, how do you find out where another person's natal planetary positions touch yours? Simply by using the planetary tables already provided. First, make a list of where your planets are for your basis of comparison. In the case of Mars, Jupiter, Saturn, Uranus, Neptune, and Pluto, write down what sign they're in and whether they're early, middle, or late in their signs (you can tell that by seeing how close your birthday falls to the dates they entered and left the signs). In the case of the sun, write down the exact degree, using the method outlined in Chapter 6, counting from the day the sun entered your sign until you reach your birthday. Also write down the placement of your Ascendant, and whether it's early, middle, or late in its sign. That's it for your natal positions.

When you find out the birthday of the person whose chart you wish to study in relation to your own, establish all the planetary positions for that person. You do not need the exact time of birth; the day and the year will suffice (all you'll be missing will be the Ascendant). In fact, unless you want the person to suspect you of astrological manipulation (of which you are indeed guilty), don't give you hand away by asking for the exact time. If, however, you want to do a complete cycle analysis on this person, you will need the exact time, so weigh your options. I usually ask only for date and year (or inveigle them each separately for even surer cover), and then go after a time only if the synastry product looks particularly promising or dire.

Once you have both sets of positions, compare them. Jot down what planets in your birth fall in conjunction with what planets in the other person's birth, and then look them up in the following section. There you will find an explanation of the potential of the contact from both your points of view. It's strictly a two-way street, and you're looking for one of four situations, depending on what you want from the relationship:

1. Your "benefics" (sun, Jupiter, Ascendant, north node) on the other person's benefics, which will imply a mutually positive and reinforcing relationship.
2. Your "malefics" (Mars, Saturn, Uranus, Neptune, Pluto, south node) on the other person's benefics, which will give you dominance and enable you to draw on the other person's resources.
3. Your benefics on the other person's malefics, which will reverse the situation, putting you on the bottom.
4. Your malefics on the other person's malefics, which will indicate nothing in particular, except a certain similarity of career rhythm.

Obviously, 1 and 2 are astrologically positive situations relative to your chart, 3 is to be avoided at all costs, and 4 can be effectively ignored in most cases. In actual practice, you'll probably find that a lot of relationships have more than one contact point and that the nature of the contact points is mixed, so you'll have to take the sum total into consideration.

SPECIAL NOTE:

You'll notice that the planets Mercury and Venus have not been included in this book. That is because their orbits are within that of the earth and thus appear to us to remain in the vicinity of the sun and follow its cycle, having no more than an additive effect on the sun cycle. In comparison work using natal positions, however, they do have some real value. Unfortunately, their positions vary widely on a daily basis, so a useful table for them for the years 1920-2000 would require another book. The same is true of the moon, which has less value in career analysis, however. If you do possess ephemerides for that period and want to include the "inner" planets in comparisons, you should consider them benefics, with Mercury lending new ideas in all contacts, Venus bringing in money or the likelihood of it, and the moon indicating emotional attachments. Thus contact with benefics brings new ideas, greater cash flow, and positive emotion, while contact with malefics suppresses these desirable effects or causes one person to drain the other in the respective areas in which the influences fall.

List of Mutual Contacts

THE SUN WITH ● ● ● THE SUN

You both share the same birthday, and likely the same outlook on life. This can make you good comrades-at-arms, but it may also give you similar goals in life that might put you into competition. Therefore it is wise to keep this relationship one of friendship only and avoid situations where you both are striving for the same position. This person could give you some stiff competition, which might destroy the natural friendly relationship that usually comes from this kind of contact.

THE SUN WITH ● ● ● THE ASCENDANT

This is an excellent combination, and if the situation is appropriate, it can spark considerable physical as well as career attraction. The person with the sun part of this contact will usually be the inner, motivating, and driving force behind the relationship, while the person whose Ascendant is involved often serves as the physical representative in mutual business matters, personally presenting ideas, projects, and intentions that have been mutually cooked up. The sun influence represents energy and motivation, while the Ascendant influence will enable its possessor to demonstrate his skill of presentation and delivery. This relationship often occurs in husband-and-wife teams where one is the power behind the throne and the second has what it takes— education, beauty, aggressiveness, wit, experience, flexibility, depending on the profession—to put it all across to the public. Once it gets going, this is a very direct situation of mutual interdependence, so make sure you have found the "right" person before getting too heavily involved, however tempting the possibility of a relationship may seem. You don't want to get in too far and find there is a serious hitch to the anticipated "smooth sailing," such as a malefic contact that will turn the initially positive relationship into mere bait for a trap in which one or the other of you winds up getting used.

THE SUN WITH ● ● ● MARS

Depending on who's got which of the two, this can be either a very energizing and sustaining or a very upsetting kind of relationship. The person with the Mars part of the bargain will find that the other serves as a pick-me-up when things get weary and can often take over burdens when they get too heavy. Care should be exercised here and the Mars person shouldn't try to use the other as a constant workhorse or source of energy. There is often a low tolerance of anger or irritation in such a relationship, particularly on the part of the sun person, who will be glad to help out but will be quite annoyed if he or she begins to suspect exploitation. A fairly erratic and sometimes explosive relationship may develop, but great energy can be derived if the situation is kept rational and well under control. The sun person should watch out for accidental damage done to his or her projects by the Mars person, however, and should either be ready to take a few knocks or avoid getting involved in the first place. In the end, the Mars person will usually obtain the greatest benefit from the relationship and will usually, although not always, be the more aggressive of the two. Thus the natural role is for the Mars person to be the employer, and the sun person to be the employee—or some such similar ranking. When that is reversed, the employee is troublesome and it can be hard to get things done unless the employer uses a particularly strong hand.

THE SUN WITH ● ● ● JUPITER

This is an excellent combination and can be a big money winner for both parties. The person with the Jupiter influence will serve as a fountainhead of ideas and new plans for projects that have good money-making potential. The party with the sun will, on the other hand, give the ideas solidity and turn them into concrete reality.

This positioning can only backfire if both parties get so carried away with all the marvelous potential they have that they bite off more than they can chew. Before launching into something new with such a contact, stand back a little and see if the project is realistic, or if your mutual ebullience is simply painting a rosier picture than can be turned into hard facts and cold cash.

The direction in which this combination will go can be judged by the other contacts as well. If, for instance, there were also a Mars-Uranus contact, then great caution would be indicated because of the added element of rashness mixed into the brew. If, on the other hand, there were other contacts that indicated mutual benefit or even the likelihood of a cautious attitude, then you could reasonably expect the combination to lead to success, and the projects undertaken to come to fruition.

THE SUN WITH ● ● ● SATURN

Despite the malefic appearance of this combination, it doesn't have to be all bad. It depends upon the nature of the two individuals involved. Normally, other factors aside, this pairing would cause the Saturn person in the relationship to use the other as a way to break out of limiting circumstances by drawing on and perhaps sapping the other's energies. Such a situation would appear one-sided—desirable if it's your Saturn and undesirable if you're the one with the sun contact.

But that prospect is not necessarily the case. If the sun individual has a particularly rash or careless character, one in need of some restraint and prudence, then this could be an ideal contact. In effect, the extra energy and rashness could be drained off to the benefit of both partners.

I myself, being rather on the impulsive side, have found direct benefit from such relationships. I was able to lend extra energy and inspiration when needed in return for a steadier hand that held me back when I needed restriction of some sort.

Therefore, analyze the whole situation with care before deciding whether the effect of this combination is for good or ill. It could typify an oppressive relationship in which a boss sits on an employee's career while reaping the maximum benefits from the employee's work, or it could signify a situation in which the impulsive partner is restrained from ruining things.

THE SUN WITH ● ● ● URANUS

This can be a highly stimulating contact that can bring anything from startling mutual originality to a knock-down fistfight. In any event, the relationship won't be a quiet one. Neither side may be said to be permanently on top here, and what will happen between you is really quite unpredictable—except to say that it almost certainly *will* be unpredictable.

In general, each side will be a source of discovery for the other, with the sun person supplying the energy and motivation and the Uranus person holding the key to sudden new understandings and ways of looking at things. Therefore, if you work in a field where innovation is at a premium, this will be an excellent contact. On the other hand, if you are in a field where rules and regulations predominate, this situation is likely to be very disruptive.

Whatever the case, the relationship will tend to be somewhat erratic and you may find yourself grating on each other in a most annoying fashion from time to time. Whether that is a small inconvenience or a major headache depends largely upon the circumstances and other mitigating factors in the personalities involved. But as long as you are both prepared to cope with or even enjoy sudden surprises, then this relationship can be profitable, even though it may at times veer toward imprudence.

THE SUN WITH ● ● ● NEPTUNE

This contact makes for rather foggy relationships and is not advisable in fields where hard-nosed reckoning is essential. Usually the Neptune individual will not have a very clear view of either the partner or the relationship and may have substituted for reality an elaborate fantasy or sheer error.

For the person with the sun here, the partner will tend to be something of an albatross. Cooperation will be very difficult because both will be seeing entirely different pictures of the situation. In cases where either individual can be effectively manipulated, this problem can be gotten around, but it almost never makes for an even, equal relationship.

In relationships where equality is not essential or even desirable—particularly where it is an advantage for one party to adulate the other as in certain teacher-pupil relationships—this aspect can be an advantage. At least as long as the pupil doesn't discover the teacher has clay feet. In that case, everything that went before, however useful or valid, will be cast aside.

Thus this contact is one to be particularly careful about on either side—it can be enjoyable for a time, but it can lead to disaster.

THE SUN WITH ● ● ● PLUTO

This is a very difficult combination and one to be avoided on both sides unless heavy power and dominance games of manipulation are your kind of fun. If pursued, it can lead to heavy entanglements of an unhealthy kind. The person with the Pluto here will have the distinct advantage and will tend to dominate the sun partner, even without meaning to.

Conversely, the sun partner will be one down even if older and more experienced, and will never be in a secure position in the relationship unless he or she is willing to accept the position of underling. This picture often depicts the boss who bullies a particular employee, who is helpless to do anything but lie down and take it. Or it can be the employee who relentlessly schemes to overthrow his superior, using sometimes dubious means to achieve his ends.

In certain types of personal relationships this contact can be very intense and even revelatory, with each partner reaching deep into the other's soul—but if you want to experience that kind of relationship, don't mix it with your career because you'll be on the bottom for good (if you are the sun partner), or (if you're the Pluto partner) you'll be guilty of the most merciless forcible manipulation that can easily turn immoral, if not criminal.

Of course, if you've got the Pluto and Machiavelli is your behavior model, go ahead—you may well find it fun and profitable.

THE SUN WITH ● ● ● NORTH NODE

This is generally a favorable contact, but not one to be taken lightly if you're already burdened with more than you can handle. The reason is that this is a relationship that can get you involved in all kinds of new directions and projects, which you will have to be able to make room for.

Not infrequently, as with all nodal contacts, you may have the feeling that the whole thing is "fated" and you don't have real control over your circumstances in the matter—but don't let that sway you if you think this person does not have your best interests at heart. To find that out, check the other mutual contact points. This is particularly true if you have the north node, since the main responsibilities evolving from the situation will likely fall more on your shoulders than on your partner's.

In either case, if you're looking for some new action when you encounter a person with these contacts, then it is highly recommended, because chances are you'll be able to cook up something nice together and no harm will come of it. It is only a problem when you've already got a full schedule and can't handle any more. If your sun is the point involved, then you will be somewhat freer and will more likely serve to get someone moving who needed the extra boost or direction.

THE SUN WITH ● ● ● SOUTH NODE

Sun with south node is usually pretty much of a one-way trip, with a lot of giving on the part of the sun and a lot of receiving on the part of the person whose south node is involved. Therefore, if you are looking to collect, whether it be money, love, or other favors, find someone with the sun on your south node.

Although a favorable situation, it is not always very long lasting. Frequently once the gift or favor has been given, you part company and perhaps never see each other again. But if you do find yourselves in a day-to-day working situation over a period of time, you can usually count on the sun partner to be quite supportive and always available when a little help is needed.

From the point of view of the person whose sun is involved, it is also a favorable relationship because the support is seldom effortful. Often what is given doesn't require any sacrifice but is freely and joyfully passed along to someone who can really use it. This can be anything from hand-me-downs to a spare career position or job opening that can be of tremendous advantage to the receiver.

Thus it's generally a very pleasant transaction all around and highly recommended, even if what is gained is quite small. The gift, on both sides, is in the giving.

THE ASCENDANT WITH ● ● ● THE ASCENDANT

This means you both have the same area of the same sign rising above the eastern horizon at birth. In this situation there are many similarities of appearance (particularly in bone structure and skin coloration) and personality. In social situations you will be likely to display the same graces (or lack of them) and often the same mannerisms.

More important, since this puts all your planet cycle numbers in sync, you will find that you experience ups and downs and personal and career events and learning periods at the same time, perhaps to an uncanny extent. For this reason, your professional relationship will wax and wane according to your mutually experienced cycles. In an up, positive cycle you'll both be doing well and can do much to help each other, even though you may not really need help. Conversely, in a down period, neither of you will be of much use or help to the other.

Another problem may be that you will attract the same style of partners, at least initially, in both social and career contexts, so you may find yourselves in competition. Usually the competition won't persist, however, because your inner qualities, which are very different, will become apparent and the surface similarities will fade in comparison.

THE ASCENDANT WITH ● ● ● MARS

This is not a particularly recommended contact for either party. It tends to cause tempers to flare, fights to break out, and hackles to be raised. The person whose Ascendant is involved is particularly vulnerable and is likely to come out the loser in any confrontations. But then again, the possesser of the Mars is likely to get the credit for starting the fight, which can result in anything from social disapprobation to a jail term, depending on the intensity of it.

There is a special case in which this contact might be of value, and that is for individuals who need a spur to get them moving and into gear. There will be stimulation on both sides as a result of the contact, so perhaps it is of benefit to two ordinarily lethargic types.

Since the 2-year Mars cycle is associated with project renewal and job-status change, it is also conceivable that this contact will serve as a trigger during the Mars cycle influence, and as a result change the job status of the Mars individual. But such an effect could just as easily signify being fired as the result of a disagreement.

This is not usually a good contact and is therefore to be avoided or guarded against wherever possible.

THE ASCENDANT WITH ● ● ● JUPITER

This is a most excellent contact and should be sought where possible. It brings good fortune to both parties concerned and creates a partnership that is both creative and expansive in a very direct, straightforward manner. In the case of the Jupiter person, the partner's very presence stimulates new ideas and plans and also provides the first and easiest method of personally carrying them out.

On the Ascendant person's part, the partner serves as a source of new ways of making money and starting new projects, and also provides the opportunity to actively implement those new directions. It is truly a symbiotic relationship, with a lot of good accruing to both sides.

Only one thing may become problematical: a certain sense of overconfidence that will make you both take on more than you can handle, each overtrusting in the other's abilities. Take extra care to size up new commitments before you leap into them filled with a sense of your own worth. It may be that your newborn plans are excellent, but will require the help and cooperation of others to be fully realized.

Overall, though, you are likely to enjoy and benefit from this contact, so take advantage of it whenever you can.

THE ASCENDANT WITH ● ● ● SATURN

Depending on which side you're on, this pairing can be a real help or a real hindrance in a career. The person with the Saturn has a decided advantage in keeping the other person down and preventing him or her from getting in the way, particularly in social circumstances. Although this ability to restrain is an advantage at times, it engenders considerable resentment in the recipient and should only be used when really necessary.

From the point of view of the person with the Ascendant, this contact could mean suppression and inability to get views or personality across when in the other's presence. It can be a very limiting and frustrating experience, unless being held back gets you off.

There are people who need to be held back because they don't have the self-control to restrain themselves. In these cases, the contact could be very helpful, though, unfortunately, it usually will not be appreciated.

In a backhanded kind of a fashion, this sort of relationship could serve as a personality challenge, much as a No. 1 Saturn cycle does, by testing your ability to get out there and be heard, despite the presence of someone with Saturn on your Ascendant. But even in this instance, conflict will necessarily be created and bad blood engendered as a result. Although it may have benefits I know not of, I encourage avoiding it.

THE ASCENDANT WITH • • • URANUS

The Ascendant with Uranus can be a very stimulating and exciting contact, and it is usually a lot of fun, though sometimes a bit risky. For the Ascendant person, the partner is a vehicle of unusual kinds of discovery, whose character may astound and sometimes confound. It will bring out a spirit of exploration and adventure in both parties, one leading (Uranus) and one following (Ascendant) down that challenging but sometimes rocky path.

Probably this combination is better for personal relationships where the new and unusual promise greater self-fulfillment than the old, worn paths. In business this is not always the case, and to stray incautiously too far from the accepted norm can sometimes be to court financial disaster. Thus this is not a good contact for working at an established type of profession. On the other hand, if innovation is the key to success in a leading-edge field, this contact can be just the thing to put you both ahead of the market. In such a case, it will be the Ascendant person who is the vehicle or promoter and developer of the Uranus person's new concepts.

If, however, there are several other harsh, combative contacts with the individual, it will usually mean a quarrel and your both going your separate ways, despite the many good things you may have learned from each other.

THE ASCENDANT WITH • • • NEPTUNE

This is usually an inauspicious contact for anybody involved in normal business transactions. It very much prevents either party from seeing or feeling what's going on in the other's mind, and hence leads to all kinds of incorrect assumptions, confusions, and often accusations of deceit where none was actually committed.

As with Neptune with the sun, the only major exception is relationships that feed on illusion, such as teacher-pupil or guru-follower. Perhaps certain facets of the entertainment business, in which illusion plays a large part, may also benefit from this contact, but few other areas will.

The exception is romantic relationships. There, the Neptune-Ascendant crossover tends to make for very devoted, star-crossed lovers who may never really see what the other is like, living instead on a self-created image, usually a far better one that either could in reality sustain. It lends itself to imitation of dime-store romance-novel relationships.

For some, such an experience may be the height of ecstasy, but if you attempt to mix that kind of pleasure with business, you're going to be in troubled waters. If you must deal with an associate with this contact, try to find another person you both trust to serve as a go-between so that matters can be kept clearer and more defined than they ordinarily might become. This precaution could save both your money and your friendship.

THE ASCENDANT WITH ● ● ● PLUTO

This is as awful a contact as you can come by and is to be avoided by anyone who does not want to become the victim of social power plays that often wreck or set back a career—and by anyone shunning the other end of the stick: making such a victim of somebody else.

The possesser of the Ascendant here is usually strictly on the receiving end, and will frequently find the other magnetic in a mysterious sort of a way, a way that almost involuntarily leads to subjugation. It creates a confrontation of wills in which one side has very little hope of winning. That is why you shouldn't get involved to begin with. Once involved, you will find it very hard to extricate yourself. A boss with the Pluto side of this contact can turn your office into a personal concentration camp built especially for you.

If you find yourself on the dominant end of this contact, don't use it on anyone you wouldn't want for an enemy, because that's the effect it will likely have in the end, unless the person is a thorough-going masochist. That's not an impossibility, as this contact has been frequently observed in cases of sexual sadomasochism—a scene that may be a turn-on in the bedroom, but doesn't belong on the job.

THE ASCENDANT WITH ● ● ● NORTH NODE

This is a challenging contact. It may almost seem as if you were put on earth to get involved with each other. Chances are, that's just what you'll do, on a larger or smaller scale, by stimulating each other into action. This is a good omen in business, where prolonged inaction leads to bankruptcy. On the other hand, if you are swamped with work a little extra action is probably the last thing you want to hear about.

This is particularly the case for the person with the north node involved, because that person will take on most of the responsibility for the commitments made and so will assume the lion's share of work. The person whose Ascendant is involved may simply walk away or be a passive recipient in the affair.

This can be an ideal situation for an entertainer or show biz personality (Ascendant) and a manager or agent (north node). In such a case, the success and popularity of one is brought on by the hard work and commitment of the other, but both benefit from it—though not equally. Therefore, give it a second thought before you put your commitments on the line with this contact. You may find that you are getting into a one-ended deal that will require a lot of work before you get a substantial payoff. On the other hand, if you've picked a winner, you could go all the way.

THE ASCENDANT WITH ● ● ● SOUTH NODE

This is a particularly tricky and delicate contact that can have explosive results for good or ill and deserves careful watching. In general, the person with the south node involved is put pretty much at the other's mercy, and the relationship develops a certain fascination that can appear quite compulsive at times.

The south node person will definitely be on the receiving end of the relationship, and how well or ill that bodes is often determined by whether there are any other planets in the vicinity of the partner's Ascendant. A benefic here can spell a delightful episode, either personal or professional, but a malefic could mean disaster—personal loss, betrayal, or worse.

On a petty level, the south node person, if working for long periods of time with the Ascendant person, may find that individual constantly underfoot, even to the point of bringing in untoward events and debts without meaning to and with no malice intended. The bungling but well-intentioned assistant who is constantly putting his foot in your mouth and being exceedingly apologetic for it is an example that readily comes to mind. You can't hate such people, but you can't always live with them either.

Outside of the business world this contact can signify a wonderful personal gift in which destiny places just the right person in your lap. It's by no means a bad contact, just difficult to judge.

MARS WITH ● ● ● MARS

This contact indicates that your basic job-energy cycle is in sync and that you will probably rise in the world and/or undergo changing job circumstances. Thus in a bull job market it could make you the best of partners, helping each other along the way and sharing jointly profitable projects in tandem. On the other hand, in a bear market you could find yourself in cutthroat competition for the same job. Keep that in mind as your careers rise and fall, particularly if you are in the same field. If you are in complementary professions, however, such as editor and publisher, copywriter and art director, then you may find that you are able to help each other in hard times.

In a situation where projects are not cyclical but very day-to-day, this shared position can be less than ideal because you'll both tire of the scene at the same time (when Mars is at its low cycle) and tend to neglect work jointly. In such a situation opposite Mars positions would be better, as one would always serve to stimulate the other, being in opposite cycles at all times.

In general, however, this is a pretty nice contact, because it gives you the same approach to getting a job done and saves on mutual style adjustment.

MARS WITH ● ● ● JUPITER

This is a very-high-energy contact and should have you both going full steam on any project you undertake jointly. New ideas will be developed quickly and much pressure will be brought to bear to continue producing at a high level.

In general, this will make for a very aggressive kind of relationship and is best suited to those who are comfortable with that style. Where both are more inclined to a "laid-back" style, the contact can become an annoyance because both partners have to put out more energy than they would prefer—though in some instances this would probably do them good.

Although this contact can spur greatly increased mutual production, with plans and ideas coming usually from the Jupiter person and energy from the Mars person, problems can arise. First, production may outstrip the capabilities of the workers' performance, thus blocking the flow of expansion. Keep a close eye on other colleagues to see if they are able to keep pace—if they aren't, slow down a bit till they catch up. Second, production can outstrip demand, leaving you with diminished rewards for your efforts.

Another possibility is health strain brought on by too much pressure. Be ready to take a break now and then, for everybody's sake.

MARS WITH ● ● ● SATURN

This, like all Saturn contacts, can go well or ill for both parties, depending upon the position they both are in and how they decided to handle each other. The individual with Saturn may tend to suppress the efforts of the other, sapping that person's energy and using it for his own ends. Such an effect illustrates a negative, one-way form of the contact, and when it seems to be occurring, a shift should be made if possible.

The positive side of the matter occurs when the Saturn individual serves to bank the fires of the more impulsive Mars person, thereby coaxing the flames of rashness and wasted energy into a steadily glowing fire of perseverance. At the same time, the Saturn person may enjoy the vivifying effects of the Mars person, and they may mutually benefit from each other's characteristics where they most closely meet.

How can you tell which is going to happen? Mainly by experience, but also by whether other mutual contacts tend toward the positive or negative. Mutual Pluto or Neptune contacts would not bode well, while some supportive sun or Jupiter points could indicate that the relationship would tend toward a balance rather than exploitation and dominance.

MARS WITH ● ● ● URANUS

This is a highly volatile contact and can result in all varieties of conflict and clatter between you, unless you are extremely well attuned and have a very precise sense of timing. Because so few people do, it usually results in rashness, contentiousness, and unexpected splits that tend to have a destructive effect on all concerned. Even when both parties are fairly level-headed and rational, these qualities may suddenly be lost and impulsiveness may take over to the detriment of both.

When the two individuals are particularly in tune with each other, and for professions in which "quick shooting" is crucial to success, this can be a good and even essential contact. Few everyday business occupations or professions answer to such a description, though perhaps as the world goes into a period of increasing turbulence this influence will be felt more strongly. Certainly it is a necessary trait in combat, and conceivably it could be an asset for buyers in the swift and hectic commodity exchange.

In most areas, however, such a contact would need to be seriously tempered by more supportive, reinforcing contacts that would encourage responsibility, in order to defuse the contact of its more troublemaking properties. Unless you like life in the fast lane, leave it alone.

MARS WITH ● ● ● NEPTUNE

This is generally a very poor contact for most career and business affairs and should be left strictly alone or minimized whenever possible. Its effect is to make the actions of one party (Mars) completely incomprehensible to the other (Neptune). And conversely, the Mars party will never be able to make a sure and certain contact with the Neptune person. In almost any situation one would normally come across, such results would not bode well for the future of a relationship.

However, there are a few conceivable instances in which this relationship could be useful, as in sending a Neptune person to defuse or deactivate a person with such a Mars contact. Conversely, one might send an overly assured and self-confident person (Neptune) into battle with someone whom he or she simply can neither pin down nor deal with (Mars) in order to provide a needed lesson in humility.

This combination can also be of use in business situations where deceitful acts are thought necessary, but I believe that such trickery is playing with fire. Misleading others so often leads to misleading yourself that it is not worth it in the long run.

MARS WITH ● ● ● PLUTO

This is a most strenuous and competitive contact and tends to put both parties at a disadvantage. People whose planets interact in this fashion frequently would be better off going their separate ways.

Usually, as might be expected, the person with Pluto involved will be at a distinct advantage, but only at the price of having to continually suppress the other. It is a steep price to pay for victory when one's adversary becomes one's obsession.

Similarly, the person with Mars involved may be defeated but will remain undaunted, so that the conflict may go on, at a smoldering level, indefinitely, causing both great energy loss and psychic harm. In a normal business relationship, that of free competition, this contact will very seldom come to any good; on a grander scale, it has the overtones of restraint of trade, and that doesn't help work very much on either side.

As with Neptune, it might be a good contact to have in an instance such as sending a soldier (so to speak) to vanquish one of your enemies, or teaching some recalcitrant colleague a lesson, but here again, we are devolving into Machiavellianism (as so often happens with Neptune and Pluto), and I believe such practices are best left out of business. They come back to haunt you in the long run, and the short-run gains just aren't worth it, in my opinion.

MARS WITH ● ● ● NORTH NODE

This is not a very favorable contact and frequently invokes considerable efforts whose fruits are wasted in the long run. The most vulnerable person is the one with the north node involved; that person may find that the other quite unintentionally ruins projects in which they are both involved, but it is the north node person who will suffer the most.

A good example is of a record producer I know who went into the studio to cut an album for the Bicentennial. It was a rush job; he had just enough time to get it on the market before July 4. Unfortunately, the engineer (who also owned the studio) had his Mars on the producer's north node, which caused the producer some consternation, but there was no time or money to see another studio and engineer.

Everything went deceptively smoothly—the album was recorded and mixed without a hitch. Then, when the time came to cut the master disc in another, better studio, it turned out that the master tape was very badly distorted, although the distortion had been impossible to hear or spot in the original studio. It was too late to rerecord the whole thing, so it had to be put out in an accoustically truncated form to minimize the distortion, thus effectively destroying the quality and presence of the performance.

The producer suffered the most—he had a wasted album—but the engineer suffered, too—he came out of it with a diminished reputation. This is not a recommended contact.

MARS WITH ● ● ● SOUTH NODE

This contact is sheer trouble and should be avoided if at all possible. The south node is a most sensitive spot, and putting an aggressive planet like Mars here is more than likely going to bring harm to the person with the south node involved. In fact, it puts this person literally at the mercy of the Mars individual, so it should be handled with extreme care on both sides.

On the one side, being so open to possible, even unintentional, damage is a very shaky position to be in. On the other side, having the responsibility for possibly harming someone is a touchy position to be in. Unless the harm is intentional, that is. This is an excellent position to be in from the Mars point of view if your aim is to rake the other person over the coals. But to know yourself the cause of harm when you didn't mean it is a tragedy.

A good example is the case of a salesman with Mars on the south node of his district manager. They were the best of friends, but the salesman did such a good job that the company fired the manager and replaced him with the salesman. Both were shocked, and the salesman was mortified—but it was a little more than their friendship could take.

A lot of nodal contacts have this kind of "fated" quality where it seems as if you just can't escape them, but I highly recommend at least giving it a try.

JUPITER WITH ● ● ● JUPITER

With most colleagues you're likely to meet, this means you were born within about a year of each other, or your ages are multiples of 12 years apart. It's really not a terribly meaningful contact, except that you may have a certain similarity in style when it comes to producing and handling new ideas and projects.

It may also mean that your general fortunes and cash-flow situations will tend to rise and fall together. Certainly your overall creativity, when it comes to developing and expanding your careers, will be more or less in tandem in the long run, although your opportunities to exploit that creativity may not be linked at all.

How close a link there may be can be pinpointed by examining your mutual cycle graphs. If they run fairly close, then you may find that you can work very well as a team. Conversely, if they run more or less opposite, you can use the overall creative similarity as an opportunity to help each other out by one using the other's talents when he or she is in a down cycle and the other in an up cycle.

In the case where one is significantly older than the other, the younger one can learn a lot from the elder about prudent and effective methods of career expansion and development, and can find out what pitfalls to avoid in the future.

JUPITER WITH ● ● ● SATURN

This is generally not a good contact, yet in the right circumstances it can go a long way toward stabilizing and sustaining a relationship. If other positive contacts are lacking, the Saturn individual will simply dampen the Jupiter person's plans and serve as a career block, while benefiting from the plans and ideas of the Jupiter person. Needless to say, given the choice, one would want to be the Saturn person here.

If other good contacts are present, however, and the Jupiter person is a bit too volatile while the Saturn person could use some pepping up, then this can be the most beneficial of relationships. I have personally found this to be the case with my closest partner, my wife, Christine. She has Saturn right smack dab on my Jupiter, so by standard classical interpretation she ought to be poison for my career. But the real effect is quite to the contrary—she tends to help rein in my rash impulses and often forces me to develop an idea more fully and properly before rushing out into the marketplace with it. That always got me into trouble before, but thanks to the effect of this contact, it's not nearly so much of a problem.

Thus, judging this contact is often a matter of judging the characters of the persons involved and deciding whether this kind of influence would be helpful or hurtful to either or both.

JUPITER WITH ● ● ● URANUS

This can be a very dynamic and profitable contact for both parties involved if they are relatively stable individuals with good business judgment. The contact lends tremendous originality with broad creativity and productivity. If this is balanced by experience and the knowledge of how to see a project through in all its details, then this can be an excellent and profitable relationship.

If, however, personal stability or experience is lacking, it can tend to cause things to fly off the handle and projects to be sent off in a half-baked state. When this happens, it will usually be the person whose Jupiter is involved who incurs the most damage, so if that person happens to be you, use extra caution.

As is always the case with Uranus, this contact is most profitable in fields where originality and creativity are highly in demand. It lends itself to broad, sweeping concepts that spring full-blown from the mind, which is why the ability to tend to details is so important. Counterbalancing and completing the dynamic but rough initial picture will obviously be of great importance in such a situation.

Where there are other, more negative contacts, this combination can often lead to quarrelsome disagreement, so in such cases it is to be avoided.

JUPITER WITH ● ● ● NEPTUNE

This is a better personal than business contact, unless you are in the "business" of ideals and spirituality (which a lot of people seem to be in these days). Its result is mutual stimulation of ideals and principles of right and wrong, and thus it can be a very enjoyable and uplifting experience on a personal level.

On a business level, however, it tends toward a lack of clarity in developmental direction or even out-and-out misunderstanding concerning where you both mean to go. This tends to cripple your forward motion, and can get you both lost in the woods as your finances slowly dwindle.

If neither of you bears financial responsibility in the involvement, you can serve as a good weathervane for where the market is going and where any given person or company within it should ideally go. But the running of day-to-day matters should be done with someone with a more solid set of contacts in relation to your planets, or simply by an entirely different third party.

Socially, this contact is quite pleasant and often very thought-provoking. Frequently the partners have a mutual admiration because they respect each other's ideals and standards. In many cases, however, this contact should be left at the social level and business pursued with others, lest business failure spoil a good relationship.

JUPITER WITH ● ● ● PLUTO

This is a very powerful contact and usually a hard one to handle. It doesn't often come up positive, so avoid it if possible, particularly if you're on the Jupiter side of the fence. In such a case, the Pluto person would easily be able to kill off all your plans for career development and expansion. It can be the supervisor who turns a deaf ear to everything you suggest, or a powerful adversary who simply crushes you in competition.

On the other hand, if you're holding the Pluto in the contact, you've got your hands on someone you can easily wipe out if you want or need to. Unfortunately, you will probably have that effect whether or not you mean to, which is something you could well regret.

In rare instances, this can indicate two persons who get together for the purpose of perpetrating a heavy power play where both influences are directed outward at another in order to mutually eliminate a competitor. Such alliances are dangerous, and the person with the Jupiter may do well to suspect that once the dust has settled, he or she will be the next victim and will be able to do little in the way of self-defense.

If you don't mind playing with fire, this can be a compelling and almost inviting contact at times, but if you'd rather not risk your own undoing, stay away from it.

JUPITER WITH ● ● ● NORTH NODE

This is an excellent contact and highly recommended, particularly if you want to put some new movement into your life. The one with the north node involved is the most favored, being provided with profitable new directions by the other, which can sometimes become a full-time occupation.

The Jupiter half of the contact benefits mainly from the opportunity to express creativity and also from finding someone who will actually undertake the ideas expressed and turn them into concrete reality. Thus, this might be an ideal relationship for an idea person (Jupiter) and a company owner (north node) who has the wherewithal to realize the ideas profitably.

Of course, the contact usually doesn't present itself on such an ideal or grand level. In most day-to-day situations, it simply indicates two people involved in projects where one is the instigator and the other is the factor. Usually this is a pretty enjoyable creative contact, unless of course you're already burdened and the last thing you need is a new responsibility, however promising. In such a case, someone with Jupiter on your north node would just be a burden.

But in virtually all cases, someone with the north node on your Jupiter will provide a good opportunity you shouldn't pass up.

JUPITER WITH • • • SOUTH NODE

With this one, you can seldom go wrong. For the person with the south node involved, this can bring money, favors, friendship, and help of all sorts, great and small. It's the planetary equivalent of a Christmas bonus, so you may look forward to encountering it.

From the Jupiter person's point of view, the transaction is also one of pleasure because the giving is easy or even profitable. Very frequently it will mean that some new venture of the Jupiter person will bring good fortune to the south node individual while making everyone a bundle.

This may sound like an overly rosy picture, and to a certain extent it is. Don't interpret it to mean that you're going to hit the jackpot every time you run into someone with Jupiter on your south node. Still, something benefical and free, however minor, is highly likely to come out of this contact—unless other, negative contacts prevent it—and the jackpot is indeed a real possibility, though you may have to do a little self-promotion with the individual to get it.

On the other side of the fence, you may find that those with the south node on your Jupiter are particularly ideal partners for future projects and expansion, so don't overlook them. By doing them a favor now, you could be doing yourself one in the future.

SATURN WITH • • • SATURN

This contact means that you are either within a year of the same age or you were born 29½ years apart. In the first case, this positioning has little influence one way or another, except that you are of the same generation and therefore share certain of the ideals and prejudices of your contemporaries. With the years, however, these differences fade away and have increasingly less significance as experience and skill become the determinants of whom we deal with rather than age.

Where there is a difference of 29½ years, however, one may find that there is much to be learned from the other, particularly in the realm of basics in the profession concerned. Thus an easier teacher-student relationship may be established than with others without the contact, as immediate understanding and communication are often manifested more easily. Such relationships, particularly if other good contacts are to be found, should be treasured while they last, because there is much to give and to receive in the way of wisdom over the years, and this can be of benefit to both parties.

SATURN WITH • • • URANUS

This contact could be a somewhat upsetting one, although that effect may be just what is needed for both individuals concerned. In the case of the Saturn person, stability of position or ideas may be shaken, which can cause not inconsiderable insecurity. But there are some hidebound folks who really need a shaking up, so although painful, the contact might be beneficial.

In the case the the Uranus person, ideas and new directions may be dampened or held back by the other, who seems to act like a wet blanket on new and original thoughts and concepts. This can engender resentment and disdain for the other person's more conservative outlook, which will lead to friction. However, the Uranus person may actually need to be held back and forced to reconsider what may have been invalid concepts in the first place. But the restraint will seldom be appreciated, I'm afraid.

This contact can have positive manifestation where both sides realize their lacks and use each other to fill them in. The result can be a very keen-edged relationship that has well-developed originality and a thorough underpinning in experience and tested, reliable methods. This will only happen, however, when both sides are willing to undergo modification in the interest of achieving something significant that neither would be able, or even inclined, to accomplish alone.

SATURN WITH ● ● ● NEPTUNE

This is a generally undesirable contact that gives little benefit to either side. On both sides it has the effect of general confusion and depression, such that neither side really agrees with the other. The resulting insecurity can be a real damper in a relationship. In the case of the person with Saturn, the feeling will be that the other person is an undermining influence because of his or her beliefs and therefore is not to be trusted. This feeling is not usually actively voiced, or even thought consciously, but it engenders nagging suspicion all the same.

The Neptune person is likely to feel that the other person's style forces moves that are incompatible with certain basic principles and beliefs, and therefore will consider that person threatening and limiting. Again, this is not likely to be an articulated opinion, but rather a nebulous feeling that makes real cooperation between the two harder.

Fortunately, this contact is not a very powerful one, and other contacts between the two persons are more than likely to overshadow it. Where it is the only meeting place between the two, it is unlikely the relationship will be close or very profitable, even if circumstances maintain it for some time.

SATURN WITH ● ● ● PLUTO

This is not at all a desirable contact, as it is one that is likely to bring both parties grinding to a halt. Each side somehow blocks the efforts of the other, even if not meaning to, and thus a frustration is produced that doesn't help matters at all.

Unless intensified by other difficult contacts, this is not likely to be that powerful an influence. However, if the situation is reinforced by other difficult influences, this difficult contact could encourage development of a battle to the death for supremacy. Both sides will easily become entrenched and unwilling to give any ground. In some instances, the bitter feud may last as long as both parties are in contact.

In general, however, you will not find much intensity coming from this contact as it is simply not a very active exchange and will only be brought into play if there are other contacts involved to set it off.

SATURN WITH ● ● ● NORTH NODE

This is an unfavorable contact and you should avoid it. For the north node person, it indicates serious limitations of future prospects and the taking on of heavy and unrewarding burdens. The only real learning advantage to this situation is the development of patience and the acceptance of what are essentially unnecessary limitations.

From the point of view of the Saturn person, the responsibility of holding someone down and becoming a burden to him is not one to be envied. If it's your worst enemy, okay, but in most instances it won't be, and any enmity generated in the process will be mostly your responsibility.

Besides, in general business practice you do not really profit from holding another down. Rather a maximum of freedom encourages more money and career opportunities for everybody. Restrictive business ploys are by nature bad for business.

Sometimes, however, neither party can really help it and somehow the one always manages to bring the other grief, with no ill intentions. One person may continually find himself a liability, so the best policy is to separate as quickly as possible so that no more damage is done. If, for some reason, separation is impossible, then the person with the north node can look forward to many a gratuitous burden.

SATURN WITH ● ● ● SOUTH NODE

This dreary contact is best avoided at all costs, particularly if you are the person whose south node is involved. The other person will bring down on your head all manner of grief, restriction, and woe—and you will be able to do almost nothing to protect yourself. It is as though that person were put in the world for the sole purpose of persecuting you. The only possible instance in which this contact could be at all beneficial is when someone requires the strictest disciplining and truly deserves what he gets.

From the Saturn side of the fence, one becomes a messenger of woe that I hardly think would be pleasant, unless one has the personality of a prison guard. As with other nodal cases, the delivery of difficulties may not be at all intentional, which makes this a doubly sorrowful situation for the one responsible. Such a relationship is not enviable and prompt disengagement is the best policy. Where that is not possible, duck.

This may seem like an overly dire prognostication. However, if there are positive contacts that will at least partially defuse this relationship, its effect will be comparatively minor. But put it together with some real negative contacts and someone (or two) had better run for cover.

URANUS WITH ● ● ● URANUS

This means that you are within 2 or 3 years of each other in age and therefore share some age-group similarities in style, particularly attitudes toward innovations and new concepts. Aside from those similarities and a certain amount of generational cohesiveness, it really doesn't have much significance. You are likely to go through similar life crises at around the same time (also a function of age), but as a one-to-one contact for relationships, this is neutral.

URANUS WITH ● ● ● NEPTUNE

The effect of this contact operates more in the realm of principle than of active conflict or cooperation, and will most notably be one of age and philosophical difference. Subjects that the Neptune person takes on faith the Uranus person will insist on exploring factually and exposing in detail. So far as personal values are concerned, this divergent outlook creates contention, but in business matters, if both parties are fairly realisitic, this tempermental conflict should never really come into play. If anything, the Uranus person will be at a bit of a disadvantage, being able to clear up confused issues for the other person, while at the same time getting his or her own clarity a bit muddied. Not that notable a contact.

URANUS WITH ● ● ● PLUTO

Like Uranus-Neptune, this aspect chiefly signifies a difference in creed or fundamental universal beliefs. Unless you are involved in the religious business—or one of you looks upon business as a religion—this contact shouldn't have much effect on everyday business life, barring emphasis from other planets on the same spot. Essentially, in the business sphere it means that one person breaks through barriers with a lightning assault (Uranus), while the other prefers a slow attack of overwhelming force (Pluto). Not all that important.

URANUS WITH ● ● ● NORTH NODE

This can be a challenging and stimulating contact, influencing the development of new and revelatory projects, but it should be handled with care because if you allow yourself to get caught up in the energy it generates, or if you take it for granted, it could lead to disaster or the sudden demise of your plans.

Usually the north node person is more subject to danger here, but I have seen some exciting though risky ventures started and successfully completed because of this aspect. Usually the Uranus person will be the motivator, while the north node individual will undertake the responsibility for acting. You can lose your shirt with this one, but you can have a hell of a good time doing it. One the other hand, if your business is a conservative one, forget it.

I have also seen some very exciting and unusual love affairs come out of this one, because, I suppose, risky love is often the most exciting kind.

URANUS WITH ● ● ● SOUTH NODE

This one is like getting kicked in the pants—or kicking someone else in the pants. For the south node person, it can be a quite painful and upsetting experience, while the Uranus person, if so inclined, may get a thrill from it.

In any event, it will make for a fairly volatile situation that, in the personal realm, might be interesting or even exciting. For a career, however, it's strictly bad business.

This contact is not likely to manifest heavily, however, unless there are some other negative contacts. This gives the possibility rather than the likelihood of sudden, disturbing action. Unless you see some other reasons for worry, this one will probably keep still.

NEPTUNE WITH ● ● ● NEPTUNE

This is another generational indicator, meaning you were born within a few years of each other and thus share some of the overall beliefs of your generation. On an individual basis, it has little meaning.

NEPTUNE WITH ● ● ● PLUTO

This contact is usually marked by a significant age difference and therefore is flavored with basic differences in beliefs, such as which principles are fundamental in life and which aren't. Its sphere of influence is personal belief. If it has any implication in the business world, it would be the tendency for one to overcome an adversary by diplomacy or deceit (Neptune) in a situation in which the other would prefer to do the job with sheer brute power (Pluto).

NEPTUNE WITH ● ● ● NORTH NODE

This is a shifty contact that really isn't very good for business because it tends to lead one down blind alleys into speculative ventures. As usual, the potential for harm lies with the north node person, who will usually bear the final responsibility for everything. The Neptune party will generally encourage the speculation and cause or add to the general confusion.

In love, this can be quite another affair, leading to long, involved romantic attachments. But many of the things that make love most rewarding tend to make businesses bankrupt, so it's better to confine this kind of contact to personal affairs.

NEPTUNE WITH ● ● ● SOUTH NODE

This contact is fraught with potential fraud and deceit, but it will probably never come to light unless there are other factors substantially motivating it. However, the south node person will always be at a potential disadvantage and at the other person's mercy if that person chooses to become harmful. Therefore, in matters where trust is at a premium, this contact is best avoided, because it will always represent a seed of danger and betrayal, a peril that might not remain dormant.

PLUTO WITH ● ● ● PLUTO

This contact means you were born within approximately 10 years of each other and share the goals and destiny of your whole generation. No more, no less.

PLUTO WITH ● ● ● NORTH NODE

This is a very restrictive contact for the person with the node involved, giving the other person the capability (though not necessarily the inclination) to stop you dead in your tracks or heavily dominate your efforts and responsibilities.

Obviously, this is an advantage for the Pluto person, who will naturally be one up on his colleague, other conflicting contacts barred. If you're the paranoid type who liks to have everybody under your thumb, this might be ideal, but for most people the thought of going around with an axe over their colleagues' heads is not a pleasant one. When it occurs, you will do best to soft-pedal it.

If you find yourself, conversely, on the receiving end of Pluto, be very wary of the other person's intentions and avoid getting into heavy entanglements that may stunt your career.

PLUTO WITH ● ● ● SOUTH NODE

For the person with the south node involvement, this can be something like getting hit on the back of the head with a blunt instrument. The possibility of forceful power plays with you on the receiving end is quite distinct. These plays can come with unexpected suddenness and brutality—fair play, decency, and honor have no part here. Be on your guard at all times and avoid the contact if you can. It may never come to fruition, but you will always be the potentially helpless victim at the time and place of the other's choosing. Not good at all.

If you are on the Pluto side of the relationship, be very careful and extra considerate, because it will be easy to do harm without knowing it. Where there is any doubt, back off lest you inadvertently cause injury. You may not be able to help it, since fate cast you in a damaging role, but give it a try.

NORTH NODE WITH ● ● ● NORTH NODE

This means you are the same age or multiples of 19 years apart, and its only real tendency is to make you more likely to take on shared responsibility or responsibilities of similar natures at similar times. Likewise, you will find yourself in receipt of rewards and payoffs of a similar nature at the same time. In terms of character relationship, it really doesn't mean a thing.

NORTH NODE WITH ● ● ● SOUTH NODE

This is just the reverse of the above. You will take on responsibilities when the other is receiving rewards and vice versa. Outside of this debt-receipt polarity reversal, there is no other real significance.

An Example Comparison

Let's take an example of how two persons—call them A and B—may be compared.

Let us say A was born on January 15, 1950, and has an early Pisces Ascendant. B was born on April 4, 1945, and has a mid-Leo Ascendant.

We look up the dates in the tables and we get a lineup that looks like this:

	A	**B**
Ascendant	Early Pisces	Mid-Leo
Sun	25° Capricorn	15° Aries
Mars	Early Libra	Early Pisces
Jupiter	Early Aquarius	Mid-Virgo
Saturn	Mid-Virgo	Early Cancer
Uranus	Early Cancer	Early Gemini
Neptune	Mid-Libra	Early Libra
Pluto	Mid-Leo	Early Leo
North Node	Mid-Aries	Mid-Cancer
South Node	Mid-Libra	Mid-Capricorn

By drawing lines between the same positions on the two columns, we find we have a formidable six-point contact between the two persons. This convergence of forces will very likely influence the depth of their involvement—the more contacts, the more involvement, as a general rule. The fewer the contacts, the less likely the involvement, and you'll find you have less intense relationships with the people with whom you don't share contact points. These people tend to drift away and prove relatively unimportant to you, as opposed to those with whom you share numerous and vital planetary contacts.

Now, let's break the list down and analyze just what type of contact we are dealing with so we can understand the type of relationship that will tend to develop between these two.

A		**B**
Ascendant	with	Mars
Pluto	with	Ascendant
North Node	with	Sun
Mars	with	Neptune
Saturn	with	Jupiter
Uranus	with	Saturn

The Ascendant-Mars contact is not all that good, sparking possible flareups, but B has the malefic "advantage" and so wins the first round.

Pluto with Ascendant is very intense, giving A a very dominant position over B, so A wins round two hands down.

The north node with sun is excellent, but also gives another round to A.

Mars with Neptune is usually difficult, though not all that intense, and this one goes to B with the malefic.

Saturn with Jupiter could possibly be a positive influence, but with the scale tipping so heavily in favor of A that the chances are it won't be favorable here and will heavily suppress the aspirations of B. Another round for A.

Finally Uranus with Saturn isn't all that significant, though perhaps it may help B cope with A's dominance, so we'll give this last, less important round to B.

The final score is three rounds apiece, but the match easily goes to A, the heavy, by a decision. The Pluto-Ascendant and Saturn-Jupiter one-two punch are just too strong to be overcome, particularly when there is advantage to be gained from B in the form of north node with sun. All B can really do is bluster and threaten (Mars-Ascendant) and try to confuse or retard the adversary (Mars-Neptune, Uranus-Saturn). The fact that B is 5 years older might add weight, but in an equal fight from equal positions, B wouldn't stand a chance. In fact, even if B began as a superior, the chances are that before long A would have managed an ouster and B would be on the street or out to pasture.

This is a particularly hostile picture, although not atypical of big-corporation politics. One would prefer more harmonious contacts, which would engender greater happiness and creativity on all sides, but that isn't always the winning approach.

Let us say, then, that poor B has been effectively given the boot by the ruthless coporate climber A and is on the street looking for a job. After sending out a stream of résumés, two offers arrive in the mail, one from C and one from D.

This time B is going to be a little more careful and do a comparison before deciding which person to work for. Upon obtaining the birth data of C (April 5, 1944, early Aries Ascendant) and D (July, 1942, mid-Leo Ascendant) by some roundabout method, the comparison looks like this:

	C	B	D
Ascendant	Early Aquarius	Mid-Leo	Mid-Virgo
Sun	16° Aries	15° Aries	10° Cancer
Mars	Early Cancer	Early Pisces	Early Leo
Jupiter	Mid-Leo	Mid-Virgo	Early Cancer
Saturn	Late Gemini	Early Cancer	Early Gemini
Uranus	Early Gemini	Early Gemini	Early Gemini
Neptune	Early Libra	Early Libra	Late Virgo
Pluto	Early Leo	Early Leo	Early Leo
North Node	Early Leo	Mid-Cancer	Early Virgo
South Node	Early Aquarius	Mid-Capricorn	Early Pisces

There are seven contacts with C and with D. Now, looking at the nature of contacts with C, this is what we get:

C		B
Jupiter	with	Ascendant
Sun	with	Sun
Mars	with	Saturn
Uranus	with	Uranus
Neptune	with	Neptune
Pluto	with	Pluto
South Node	with	Pluto

This lineup is completely favorable to B, particularly highlighted by the excellent Jupiter-Ascendant combination. Dominance is achieved in the Saturn-Mars and Pluto-south node, though the latter should obviously be soft-pedaled—if you come on as dominant to a prospective boss, you'll never be hired. This combination bodes well for B, but now let's look at the other lineup:

D		B
Ascendant	with	Jupiter
South Node	with	Mars
Jupiter	with	Saturn
Mars	with	Pluto
Saturn	with	Uranus
Uranus	with	Uranus
Pluto	with	Pluto

This combination isn't bad either, but the results are more mixed. Ascendant-Jupiter looks good for both, but south node-Mars, Jupiter-Saturn, and Mars-Pluto give B far too much dominance and restrictive power over the prospective boss. If B wanted to repeat A's cutthroat tactics, then this would be the employer to choose—someone who can be walked all over and used to achieve ulterior career ends.

On the other hand, if B chose C, the work might be a little bit harder (Mars-Saturn), but the atmosphere would probably be a lot more convivial, with employer and employee more likely to rise together and remain friends. Notice that in both comparisons the generational contacts (mutual Uranus, Neptune, and Pluto) have been ignored as essentially meaningless.

Which will B choose? That will depend on the character and ambitions of our job-hunting friend. If it were you, what would *you* do? Many other factors should enter in at this point: Which job is more interesting? Which has more prestige? Which pays more?

Even after the selection has been made, other influences will affect it. If B chose the situation where heavy dominance was possible, it could be a bad move because D might be savvy enough to size up a cutthroat climber right away and fire the new employee the next day. On the other hand, C could be the type who doesn't really want to work on a one-to-one creative basis, so the good contacts could be largely wasted.

As I have repeatedly stated, planetary cycles and contacts are by no means a sure key to success, but they have sufficient weight at times that they should not be ignored. If B had known the trouble A was eventually going to cause, B could have done something about it in the first place and not been muscled out of the first job.

This is a particularly extreme example to demonstrate the comparison process clearly. In most cases, your choices won't be so delineated and you may not have the freedom to pick whom you want to work with. In addition, you will be working without the Ascendant much of the time, which can often make the difference, though it didn't affect these example decisions markedly.

Throughout, you will have to take into account the position of the other individual relative to yourself—superior, equal, or inferior in job status. You will also have to size up your own style in relation to how you want to rise in your profession and relative to the style of the profession itself. I myself prefer to stick to mutually beneficent contacts, as they give a more pleasant work atmosphere and everybody's happier in the long run. But then I'm in a business where pleasant contacts can be established and a living can still be made. Some corporate styles are such that nice guys really do finish last, and there you have to use any planetary weapon you can get hold of just to stay alive.

There you have it. By using the cycle-charting methods, along with the comparison techniques, you can provide yourself with a kind of radar that can be of great help in steering around the reefs in the stormy sea of fortune. It can also often tell you where the calm, productive waters lie. Use this knowledge in good health, and you will prosper.

You will, that is, if your ship is well rigged and you know a bit of seamanship. That rigging and sea-readiness, the basic tools of job-getting and career formation, are what the next and last chapter is about.

BACK TO BASICS:
PRACTICAL CAREER BUILDING
WITH THE AID OF CYCLES

So far, we have discussed a number of different techniques for viewing your career that will give you an advantage over those who do not know them. However, they are of little use if you do not have an effective overall plan of operations within which to employ them. Thus it is necessary to look at some of the ways such a plan can be structured.

The sad truth is many people don't have any sort of strategy or superstructure worked out. They just drift from one job to another, wherever the wind leads them, somewhat like a ship with flapping sails. Others seem to pick a direction at random, perhaps because it looks financially promising, and pursue it without realizing they may be headed in the wrong direction as far as their whole life is concerned. Such a choice may lead to misery or ruin farther down the road.

Therefore, before launching yourself in any direction, it is wise to sit down and analyze (1) your talents and interests; (2) your personal and lifestyle requirements; (3) careers that are available that satisfy the first two requirements, what talents, knowledge, and so forth you will need to be successful in the area you choose; and (4) the cycle periods you are in. Such analysis is valuable whether you are just starting out, considering changing your career, or are fairly settled but want a better view of things.

1. TALENTS AND INTERESTS

It is a good idea to take stock of these factors, even to the point of making a list. You may find out there's more to you than you thought. You may have already and, unbeknownst to you, have developed certain skills and familiarities that, when combined, qualify you for directions you had not previously considered. Mathematical ability, for instance, can lead you to other things besides a job in accounting or teaching math. Combine such a skill with a fascination for risks and forecasting, and what do you get? Jimmy the Greek! In this rapidly changing age you never know where your skills and inclinations will lead you, so do not restrict yourself to traditionally delineated careers when there may be new areas opening up that will suit your particular blend of talent and interest. In fact, if you find nothing immediately available that really suits you, you may be able to create a new field for yourself. All the recently created careers, from ecologist to professional psychic, were started by someone—and the next one may be started by you.

2. PERSONAL AND LIFESTYLE REQUIREMENTS

A career is simply a set of endeavors that, ideally, supplies personal happiness and satisfaction. In this respect, a career should serve you, not the other way around. Unfortunately, all too many people are slaves to their careers, which, because they choose unwisely, force them to live in a fashion that provides them with money, but not personal satisfaction. Therefore, take stock of yourself: What do you really want out of life? A lot of money? Prestige? Creativity? To make a contribution to history? There are careers that can get you one or more of these, so you should choose accordingly. If your goal in life is to live in the country in a big house with a large family, you will have to get something that will eventually lead to a fairly large income. If your real happiness comes from working at some creative pursuit that continually changes and offers new challenges, you may have to sacrifice the large financial gains that duller jobs might net you. If prestige is your goal, again it may actually cost your money. A private-school teacher, for instance, has more presitge than a garbage collector, but the garbage collector often makes more in.both wages and benefits.

A lot of people, particularly since the early sixties, want to feel that they are doing something to change the world for the better, thus leaving their mark on history. This need has generated all kinds of low-paying jobs, from social worker to consumer advocate, that have a high yield in "soul satisfaction." Satisfaction comes in many forms, so weigh them all before choosing your direction.

3. AVAILABLE CAREERS

Now that you've got some idea of what you want and what your potential is, size up the possible careers that meet both. Investigate what training is necessary to enter them, and also how limiting they might be if you should ever want to get out of them. Some professions die on you because of oversupply of labor or dwindling demand, so what looks like a secure spot now may be very shaky by the time you're in it. A couple of examples come to mind. In the early and middle sixties both folk and pop music were enjoying tremendous growth. There was a large demand for those types of music and not a big supply of musicians to fill it. Thus practically anybody who could strum a guitar could get paid to do it (you didn't even have to know how to sing—Bob Dylan proved that). The result was that thousands of persons flocked to the field, and before you knew it, there were more proficient guitar players around than you could shake a stick at. In 1970 styles began to change and actual record and music sales dropped off sharply, and all of a sudden there were a lot of people on the street with guitars who couldn't get hired anywhere. What was worse, their musical training and experience suited no other profession, so they became virtually unemployable unless they were willing to start from the beginning and retrain.

The same situation occurred with city employees as a result of the massive layoffs during New York City's fiscal crisis. Laid-off police could often find jobs as private guards or private investigators because of their training, although there were not enough of these jobs to go around. Teachers had a college degree, which gave them entree into various new careers. But firemen found their experience virtually useless, and they had to start over entirely to keep from starving.

This kind of shakeup can happen in almost any field, so try to pick a career in which your back won't be against the wall if you are laid off or if you find that you don't really like it and want to move on to something else.

4. CAREER CYCLES

There is a fourth factor you will be able to look at, which most others will not have at their disposal unless they have read this book. That is your career cycle rhythm. Look at your twelve different cycle charts and see what the overall picture for the future is. If your No. 2 cycle is on the downswing (more Saturn than Jupiter), don't launch into something for which you will have to depend on immediate cash flow, such as your own business. If you do, you're asking for a rougher time than necessary and perhaps total failure. Similarly, if your chosen area depends upon immediate creativity, your No. 5 cycle had better be in positive shape or the wellsprings of inspiration could run dry before you're established. The example of the lawyer, previously mentioned, is what can happen if you don't take these factors into account. See what your optimum cycles are for the next few years, and then see if you can find an area where they matter and can help pull you ahead of the competition. If you can find such a career that is to your liking, then you will be in especially good shape. Going into personal sales when you're headed into a high No. 1 cycle is a good example.

If, however, sales just doesn't fit your style or goals, don't let the cycle push you into something you're going to regret. Find something more to your taste that can be helped by a high No. 1 cycle, or at least avoid areas that would waste it entirely (such as something restrictive, like law or medical school). Ideally, since cycle peaks tend to occur in rhythmic succession, you should find an area that entails periodic shifts in training and work demands that roughly coincide with your cycle peaks in those areas. That way you'll always be riding the tide.

Training

The more training you have, formal or informal, the better off you will be and the more freedom of choice you will have in your career. Training of the wrong kind or training displayed to the wrong people can actually do you harm, however, so you have to watch out. If your training and subsequent experience are too specialized—as was the case with the musicians and firemen—you may find yourself at a dead end. On the other hand, training that should be helpful in many business endeavors, such as typing and secretarial skills, could prevent you from getting promoted beyond the job level where these skills are essential.

Any kind of training will go faster and better in a Jupiter No. 6 or No. 12 cycle when important external efforts are usually dormant. A Saturn No. 6 or No. 12, however, will turn most training into a grind and a bore, and a Jupiter No. 1 will have you chafing at the bit, wanting to get out and make things happen. The first kind of training that most people consider is, of course, college. Until the sixties that was considered a *sine qua non* for a successful career in business, despite the fact that few of the corporate giants who industrialized this country had college educations. Then, as the so-called counterculture developed over the next 15 years, it became evident that there were many things people could do that didn't fit into the establishment and certainly didn't require a degree. Some very high-paying jobs do not require a college degree, although they do involve some form of training. Most large firms have systematized job-training programs that are designed to give you the skills and outlook that will be most advantageous in their particular business, and there are many trade and technical training courses available from a variety of sources that will give you practical skills that will put you ahead of someone taking the same amount of time to get a B.A. degree. Before deciding how to proceed, investigate what is available in the field or fields you would like to enter.

Of course, for many professions, such as medicine, law, education, and engineering, a university education is required by law or custom, and you won't get to first base without one. Even in business, having attended a good or prestigious school is more advantageous than picking up skills on the job. It is a primary source of connections through which you may advance yourself throughout your career.

In almost any area a college degree is a help, particularly when looking for a first job. But it may not be worth 4 or more years and tens of thousands of dollars. In journalism, for instance, 4 years of hard work on a daily paper is worth more to a prospective editor than a journalism degree because it tells him you know the business and can deliver on a deadline. The older you get, the less a degree will mean; your track record will be more important. If you didn't go to college but have a record of consistent and improving achievement, you are much better off than a college graduate whose record is only so-so. A prospective employer will be able to see you have superior talent and willpower, whereas the other person simply isn't living up to his or her education. In the long run, nothing succeeds like success.

One function college serves very effectively, particularly if it is paid for by your family or perhaps a student loan, is as a buffer period during which to decide on a career. Marking time in college is worth a whole lot more in the long run than marking the same time being a dishwasher, even if you have to pay for the former and you get paid for the latter. At college, you get an education that is bound to help you in some way, and at the same time you get a period of grace during which you can put off serious career decisions. Working in a menial job will get you nothing you can bank on later in life, and just enough to live on at the time.

The lesson here is a general one. Life should be a continual learning experience, whether formally in school or in the marketplace. Whatever you are doing, it should be something you can profit from later or something that broadens your talents and outlook. By this process you not only maximize your job potential in a given profession, you also heighten the possibility of synthesizing a profession or career for yourself that is entirely new and in which every step you take will be a ground-breaker. In our current state of economic volatility and social change, this ability is increasingly at a premium. Those who can use a variety of experience to cross traditional career boundaries will be the shapers of the future, a pursuit which is both financially rewarding and personally satisfying.

Even in the most conservative professions, it is increasingly recognized that standing still is actually sliding backward, and the wider the base of current knowledge and experience, the more valuable the executive or employee. It is only in dead-end jobs that ignorance or lack of ambition have any value, either to employer or employee. Most people get stuck in such positions at one time or another, but only those who truly deserve them remain there for long. The degree and speed with which one rises in the world is to a considerable extent a function of a wide education, not externally imposed but internally sought and dug from whatever the environment provides.

Getting a Job

Once you've decided what you want to do and have a certain amount of talent and training to qualify for it, how do you go about securing a position? There probably are about as many ways to get a job as there are jobs to get, and there are numerous professionals dedicated to helping people get jobs, not to mention all the people who make money off writing books on the subject.

This is the critical step, for what's the point of having struggled this far if you can't get a good job out of it? Unfortunately, it is impossible to hand out a good game plan that will land everyone a good job. A plan must depend on personal style, chosen profession, and type of employer. Sad to say, you will find a lot of books on career planning that have a very definite philosophy that is supposed to work for everyone. One book I know, a very popular paperback, recommends that you storm into a potential employer's office and practically grab him by the scruff of the neck to prove what a dynamic and aggressive individual you are and how indispensable you will be to the company. That approach might gladden the heart of Dale Carnegie, it might even impress certain employers today, but the chances are that you'd get thrown out on your ear or at least look like a fool.

The only solution is to reconnoitre and find out what approach is customarily successful for the company concerned. Some employers hire only through employment agencies. Some hire only on the basis of résumés received in the mail. Some want a glowing letter of self-praise telling why you're the best person for the job, and others would be offended by such a letter. Some base their judgments mostly on your personal presentation at a meeting, and others you may never meet until after you've been hired. Since the successful approach differs from place to place, you have to be flexible enough to find out what's appropriate for each situation. That means surveying the different recommended approachs and deciding which one or combination is best for any given situation.

In this respect, career cycles can help you. You'll generally find that a personal meeting is a great help if you are in a Jupiter No. 1 cycle or it is the time of year when the sun is near your Ascendant (in the same sign or in an adjacent sign). If you are in a Saturn No. 1 or the sun is six signs away from your Ascendant, then a personal meeting might do you more harm than good. If you are in a Jupiter No. 10 or the sun is ten signs from your Ascendant, a résumé will do you the most good. Conversely, if you are in a Saturn No. 10 or the sun is four signs from your Ascendant, the résumé should be downplayed.

THE RÉSUMÉ

Ah, the résumé. How do you make it up? What can it do for you, and how can it hurt you if improperly used? While there are widely divergent opinions on the proper length and style of a résumé, there are some overall general principles:

A résumé should run as long as it's interesting. If you've got a lot of accomplishments, flaunt 'em. But if you pad out your résumé with minor courses or irrelevant interests, you will probably get a boredom-induced turn-down. I favor a one-page résumé that is to the point but stimulates a person to want to find out more. In fact, I once was taken to a very expensive lunch by a vice president of a major publishing company who was interested in meeting me—he didn't have a job opening, but he was intrigued by what he read in my résumé. Incidents like that can give you some great connections, even when they don't land you immediate employment.

What a résumé should show is progress and advancement in training, experience, position, and salary. If it shows you have been stuck in the same place for a long time, employers will figure there's a good reason for that and doubt your worth. If it shows you have dropped from a higher to a lower position, either in responsibility or salary, that will raise suspicion. Each stint of employment should show regular advancement over the previous one, and a reasonable amount of time should have been served at each. If your résumé shows four or five different jobs at different companies within a short time, a prospective employer will figure you're a job hopper and you won't get hired.

Tailor your resume to the company you're approaching. This is particularly important if you have a variety of skills or experience. Use the bulk of the résumé to detail your experience and training in that company's area only, listing the rest of your talents under outside interests. Listing all you accomplishments together not only tends to confuse employers, but makes many of them suspicious. They don't like multitalented people, perhaps because they seem to be a potential threat or somehow irresponsible. A unidirectional person is thought more likely to toe the company line without conspiring against his boss. This also applies when you have been a boss yourself and are applying for a lesser, though perhaps higher-paying, position in a bigger company. Unless you downplay the power and independence of your previous position, you are a real psychological threat to your potential boss and will be turned down as "overqualified." It is a strange paradox: Employers *say* they want to hire people with ambition, but then get paranoid about anyone who seems to have been too successful.

If you have a lot of imagination and want to expend real effort on your résumé, you can make it an engaging piece of literature that can be a great help to you. I have seen résumés that are regular typeset ads for individuals, complete with graphics—they look like something out of a Madison Avenue ad firm. Usually the emphasis is on how hard the individual is willing to work and how much his or her talents would lend the company's sales picture. The point in such a case is to be splashy, but convincing. The potential employer must be led to believe that you not only have talent and experience (or training), but that you are a hard worker and will really produce for the company. After all, that is what an employee is hired for—output. The detailing of previous experience should not emphasize position and responsibilities so much as how you used these to improve the lot of the company you were working for—how sales went up, territory was expanded, or methods were improved because of what you did. You are being hired to improve the bottom line. But remember, a good résumé will be particularly useful during a Jupiter No. 10 cycle, while in a Saturn No. 10 cycle or a Jupiter No. 1 cycle, you'll be better off relying more on personal impression. Tailor your use of the résumé to fit your cycles.

Using the Job

Let us assume that your talent and résumé have landed you a job. Now what do you do with it? How do you use it to further your long-range career goals?

If it is your first job, or an early one in your career, the chances are it won't be all that exciting or fulfilling. Still, it can (and should) serve to develop your career. No matter how menial the job, it got you into the market so now you are exposed to what goes on in the field. You will see how things really work and how your superiors handle a variety of situations—situations you will be faced with someday in their positions, it is hoped. This is true in any job, from the bottom all the way up to the top.

One of the most valuable things you may get out of an early job is training. Many big companies have formal training programs that will acquaint you with the skills you will need in order to get ahead in the field. Take anything you can get your hands on—it will all help in the end, and it can make a dull job a little less boring.

In this same learning area is the experience you get from doing your job, even if it is a routine one. The better you know it and the more you can produce, the more effectively you will be able to manage an employee doing the same thing when you rise to a higher position. There is another reason for performing lesser tasks well—your reputation. If you consistently do well at whatever you're assigned, you're much more likely to get promoted than if you do a hasty or shoddy job.

This rule has certain exceptions. If you do a certain job particularly well that no one else can or will do as successfully, you may find yourself trapped in it because you have become so valuable to your boss. You may even be given raises just to encourage you to remain where you are and do the job that nobody can do. Your best way out is to provide someone else who can do it, though that has certain inherent risks (you might not get promoted, just replaced). Watch out for those jobs and try to stay out of them.

A final benefit you derive from any job you do is developing connections. You get to know people in the business whom you can tap for assistance or references for as long as you're in the business. Around you are future partners, employees, competitors, and bosses you may have at your disposal if you take the time to cultivate them now. The person who concentrates on the job alone and neglects its social context is wasting a lot of future potential.

At all times keep an eye on the varying career cycles because they will give you some good hints on how profitably things will go in which areas, when new prospects may materialize, and which prospects are real and which false. For instance, an imminent Mars return may indicate you should seek to change your job status or ask for a raise—or it may be a good time to consider changing jobs. Conversely, a Saturn No. 1 is a bad time to demand a raise from your boss.

Climbing the Ladder

Once you are fairly well ensconced in your career, you face the long and complex task of climbing the ladder to the top of your field or company. This is far too complex a subject to go into detail here, but there are plenty of books to be had on the subject—a particularly good one being *Modern Management and Machiavelli* by Richard H. Buskirk (Mentor). A few points can be mentioned here.

First and foremost, in order to succeed you usually (though not always) need to be good at what you do. All the plotting and scheming in the world won't get you to the top and keep you there unless you know your field inside out. Thus you must make your career a continual learning process if you want to keep ahead of the competition. A leading surgeon, for instance, keeps on top of the latest medical research, while many country doctors haven't learned anything new since they got out of medical school. Which do you want to be, the person who is continually working on self-improvement or the person who coasts through life? For some kinds of personalities, coasting is preferable, while others thrive on pressure and competition. Obviously, this book is intended to help those who want to get ahead in their careers, but there's nothing wrong with coasting if you can find a niche within which to do it securely. It will allow you the precious spare time you may require to follow outside pursuits that are more important to you than how you earn a living. The writer Marcel Proust, for instance, was far happier as a postal clerk than he would have been as a major corporate executive.

Being a top-notch performer is not sufficient to get you to the top, however. Many an expert and high achiever has been shot down in flames by company or professional politics. Learn to play the game, even if you don't like it or don't want to be very active in it. For the sake of survival, learn enough to defend yourself, even if you don't want to get involved in aggressive participation. Know who's got it in for whom and what person might be looking for a chance to stab you in the back. Here the previous chapter on comparisons can be of great help in spotting potential danger and potential benefits. If you're into the Machiavellian game, of course, it can be a great help in sorting out safe opponents from those who will be able to turn on you and give you a double dose of your own medicine. Despite his brilliant and conniving mind, Machiavelli was a loser in the end—but then he didn't have career cycles to work with, so you may have an advantage over him.

When dealing with an adversary, perhaps in an attempt to get his job, it is wise to take a positive approach. Don't try to do it by pointing out the person's faults to the boss or showing how he's not doing his job. Most bosses loathe character assassination of this sort, so it is more likely to get you fired instead. Remember, nobody likes a squealer, even those who profit from one. Instead, figure out ways of demonstrating that you could do the job better, perhaps by taking over part of the other person's work load under the guise of "helping out." Once it is seen that you're doing the work your competitor should be doing, the job is yours. All the planetary comparisons in the world won't help you if you can't show you are the person for the job, while playing your cards right can help you overcome the worst planetary disadvantages.

The best way to get a raise or a better position is to point out what a wonderful job you have been doing and ask for it. If your boss recognizes your efforts, you will be rewarded because such a reward is truly in the interests of the company and all concerned. A lot of bosses, unfortunately, aren't that enlightened. Some are plain stingy. Others may want to keep you where you are because you're so valuable there, and still others will figure they've got you over a barrel and there's nothing you can do about it.

There usually is something you can do. Ricardo's Iron Law of Wages says that you make no more at your present job than you could get elsewhere. Therefore, go elsewhere. Once you have a better offer in hand, you're in the ideal bargaining position. But you'd better make sure you really do have a firm offer from the outside—bluffing here is asking for disaster. For rational or irrational reasons, the boss knows just how much he or she is willing to pay you. If you're already at that limit, you could find yourself on the street in a minute. You could be surprised and crushed to find out of how little value you are to your boss.

Be careful not to jump at better offers from the outside before carefully investigating them. What looks like a golden offer could turn out to be fool's gold. A prospective employer who wants you badly enough will promise you the world. You won't find out until after you've made the move that the promising new position is slavery in disguise or offers far less security and advancement than you had been led to believe. The grass is always greener on the other side of the fence, so check it out carefully before giving up your bird in the hand.

If you do decide to make a move, do it quickly and decisively. This applies equally to a move of your own volition and an involuntary one (you're fired). The longer you take to make the change the more hostility and resentment will be built up all around, and that is to be avoided at all costs. Both firing and resigning are symbolic rejections of the individual or the company, even if the causes are clearly justified (the company ran out of money, you found a better-paying position). If you leave quickly and gracefully, you will retain your previous contacts as friends to be counted on later. If you allow hostility to occur, not only could you lose potentially valuable contacts, you could find yourself blackballed by your former employer. Therefore, resist the effort to give your employer a piece of your mind on parting, as immediately satisfying as that might be. Remain cordial—later, you'll be glad you did. Before you make any hasty leaps, look at your cycles to see if you might be jumping into hot water—such as during a Saturn No. 10 or Jupiter No. 8 cycle, where landing a truly better job might be less likely, or job hopping would tend to make you look irresponsible.

Another major division of climbing the ladder is learning to protect your rear (or cover your ass, as it is sometimes put). This is less an act of climbing the ladder than one of preventing yourself from falling, or being pushed, off it. This is usually an unspoken and even secretive talent that is essentially passive in nature though it sometimes may require elaborate precautions. It is the art of making sure you don't get the blame when somebody else screws up.

Thus when your boss makes a particularly unwise decision and asks you to implement it, make sure you have his order in writing so that if disaster results, he is clearly the source of the decision. When promises are made upon which you have to depend, make sure they're not just verbal handshake agreements, or you may find yourself holding the bag later. This is particularly the case during the No. 12 Saturn cycle, when your enemies may be marshaling forces against you without your knowledge. Whenever there is something bad going on, make sure you can prove it wasn't your fault—and when something good is going on, try your best to get your name tagged to it, even if only in a minor role, so you can use it as a credit later.

Forming Your Image

Outside of skill, productiveness, and politics, there is another factor that, perhaps unfortunately, plays a significant role in career success or lack of it. That is image. Many things go into making up your image and they can be manipulated to your advantage only if you know what they are. The first and most obvious is personal appearance—clothes, haircut, makeup, and grooming. Every industry has a dressing style that denotes the successful person. If you're not wearing some version of this style, you look like a loser, or at least an outsider, and that can seriously work against you. Accepted dress varies according to profession, from pin-striped suit to overalls for men, and from evening dresses to dungarees for women. There are several good "dress for success" books on the market for both men and women, and it wouldn't hurt to take a look at one.

Another, less immediate factor in your image is the things you surround yourself with—your home, family, possessions, clubs, and associates. The best-dressed banker who lives in a crash pad and runs around with dope smokers is suspect and can expect to get nowhere in that staid business. Conversely, hippies look silly in Cadillacs, and riding around in an El Dorado is a good way to alienate associates down on the commune.

A third, less tangible factor in image formation is your attitude. Dale Carnegie and Fulton Sheen made their careers preaching that sermon, and it is true, at least to a certain degree. If you act like a winner, on top of dressing like one and picking winning surroundings, there's a much better change you'll be one. Money attracts wealth (which is why the rich are always getting richer) and success attracts success, even if it's just pretend success at the beginning. It's easier to get work when you're already working, for instance, because you appear already successful. When you're unemployed, you'll find it harder because you look like a failure. Being aware of this and acting the part can get you a lot of extra free help, while ignoring it can only hurt you.

Since the sixties a lot of people have come to strongly object to the kind of image stereotyping that all of this advice implies. If clothes make the man, why bother to put a man inside them at all? Many people look upon the whole thing as debasing, and I certainly agree that it is. It is dehumanizing. Unfortunately, however, employers and competitors do not look at you as a person primarily (that is the function of your friends). They look at you as a potential money gain or loss, an object of possible financial reward or threat, and they judge you by the external indicators of success. Therefore, clothing, surroundings, and attitude should not be looked upon as prisons of the soul but as clever camouflage designed to manipulate your adversaries. Refusing to use these methods is like standing in the middle of an open clearing on a battlefield asking to get shot down. Capitalist society is based on competition, a free-for-all war without actual physical bloodshed. If you're not going to use the available weapons, get out of the war.

Of course, you can't really opt out altogether. We all have to be in the war to some extent or we can't make a living. Here you have to make a personal decision based on how much you like the optimum-success lifestyle, how much you are going to let these factors run your life, and how much success you're willing to give up if you don't. Stereotyped images aren't as rigid as they were before the dress and appearance revolution of the sixties, but they still have a disturbingly powerful effect both for good and bad on your career efforts. Whatever image you are trying to project, remember that its success will be greatly affected by cycles. In a Jupiter No. 1, for instance, almost any image can succeed, at least for a time, whereas in a Saturn No. 1 your ability to form a suitable image will be sorely tried.

Productivity

The mainstay of any successful career is still productivity. That means money to you and money to your employer who pays you. The more you get done, the more everybody profits, under most conditions.

Many people confuse productivity with hard work. They simply aren't the same thing. You can sweat your brow off all week behind a horse-pulled plough and not get nearly as much area ploughed as a person sitting restfully behind the wheel of a tractor. Productivity is tangible output, however you get the job done.

The key to productivity is not the amount of labor put in, but its efficiency. Time used figuring out faster and easier ways to do things is time well spent. Anything that multiplies or magnifies your effect on your environment will make your output greater and your productivity higher. The first human to pick up a rock or stick and use it as a tool or weapon discovered that fact. Recently, however, the Puritan work ethic has somewhat clouded the principle.

A lot of the work one encounters consists, at least partly, of repetitive busywork: writing letters, making appointments, taking things in and out of files. All of this takes time away from breaking new ground and getting the real money-making business done. That's why the secretary (and more recently, the personal computer) was invented. If you find yourself bogged down in busywork, beg, borrow, or steal a secretary, even if one isn't usually attached to your position. The difference in productivity will more than pay for his or her salary. Ideally, you shouldn't be doing anything but those things that only you can do and nobody else. The first quality of a leader is to be able to delegate authority well.

Don't waste time. There are so many people and schedules in this world that seem designed to keep you from getting something important done. Cut these people out of your life, at least as much as you can, and rearrange schedules for efficiency, including extracurricular activities that may cut into valuable work time.

Get tools, and get good ones. If you're a writer, for instance, don't just get a typewriter. Get a personal computer, the best one you can afford. You'll increase your speed (and therefore efficiency) and editing and rewrite becomes a breeze. If you have to work with numbers, take the same advice. If you're a traveling salesman, get a really comfortable car with all the trappings to make your driving time more comfortable so you get there refreshed. The best, most modern equipment is always worth the extra money because of the time and energy it saves you and the extra productivity that results.

Establish a work quality level that is sufficient to the task, but does not outdistance it. You can spend double the time getting something absolutely perfect when total perfection is not really required. When it's good enough, go on to something else. You need spend no more time on it as long as it is up to standard.

Use time that might be ordinarily wasted, such as travel time on a bus or subway or waiting time in a reception room. If there is no actual work you can do then, at least you can read a book or magazine that will add to your knowledge of your field. Watch your cycles. Jupiter No. 5 and No. 6 are excellent periods for improving efficiency with new methods—methods that will greatly ease Saturn No. 5 and No. 6 when they come along.

These are just a few ways to increase productivity and get ahead. There are lots of good books on improving your career efficiency, and you would do well to look at a few. Indeed, if career success is your goal, you should make a special effort to read everything of merit on the subject. For starters, I recommend Richard Buskirk's *Your Career* (Mentor paperback), which gives excellent, no-nonsense advice on the whole field. There are also specialized books that deserve attention.

Changing Careers

Before ending this "good advice" section, one important thing merits consideration. That is changing careers. There was a time when that was done only rarely. One got into a profession and stayed there, developing from beginner to master of the trade.

Today's marketplace is much less stable, however, and changing technology is creating new careers and making others obsolete at a dizzying pace. People in all kinds of work are suddenly finding the rug pulled out from under them as their field of endeavor is supplanted by another or the demand for the product they produce vanishes. In addition, many people are finding their given professions personally limiting and creatively unsatisfying, and therefore deciding to chuck them and start in with something new that holds more promise.

A lot can be done by planning ahead of time for a possible voluntary or forced career change in the future. Don't pick a narrow field that will leave you without any outside skills to draw on should it fail you. If you should for some reason prefer to be in such a field, develop alternate skills on the side, even if these be only typing and shorthand. Such skills could keep you solvent should the wolf appear at the door. Cultivate outside activities that could be used in some other career area, or at least contribute to your background if you do have to make a shift.

Suppose the change faces you without time to prepare. Then you have to sit down and take stock of your talents and background and see what you can cook up, just as you did when beginning your career. If you leaped blindly into that one, this may be the first time you have done such a self-analysis, and you may be surprised to see just how many divergent talents and interests you do have.

Naturally, it is important to take a careful look at all your career cycles to see what general areas are most favored in the time approaching. You will need all the help you can get because you will have less experience than competitors of the same age. Your career cycles give you a hidden advantage so that people will be more likely to overlook your shortcomings and focus on your talent and willingness to work and learn.

Many people have responded to the challenge of forced career change by creating an entirely new career out of a synthesis of their original career knowledge and experience with other skills and learning in a fashion that satisfies new needs in industry and consumerism.

The "counterculture," in fact, spawned hundreds of jobs and even professions no one had dreamed of before, and these are making a very good living for their creators and those that followed them. That process is still going on, as combined technologies create new and changing demands in the world at large. Those forced into career changes would do well to try to analyze current needs and trends to see if there isn't a potential, and yet untapped, gold mine waiting for them.

For the person seeking to change careers, a good deal more caution is advised. When you're out of work, you frequently have little to lose by trying a new direction. But when you've got a secure position, you're often risking everything by trying an entirely new tack. If you feel you must change careers, do it gradually so you can test your success as you go along. Don't burn your bridges behind you. Too many people have given up valuable well-paid positions on speculation, only to find that there was nothing to return to when the new venture failed. It is a better policy to slowly ease into a new career, developing new contacts, until the direction is truly tested and appears secure. Only then should you sever your ties and involvement with your previous career.

Moving On

This is not a book on generalized career advice, but one on the especially useful area of career cycles, so this is enough of common-sense knowledge. You can use your own good sense and explorative capabilities to ferret out the specific rules and principles that apply to your individual field. It is hoped that the combination of career cycles with practical knowledge of your given field or endeavor will result in an extra added success factor. Used with attention and discretion, the cycles will undoubtedly give you an advantage over your competitors.

EPILOGUE

It's a long way from the orbits of Jupiter and Saturn to the hiring hall, and yet the two seem to be linked in a statistical if not in a physical manner. What are the implications of this? Are we sinking into an age of superstition where we renounce free will and follow what the planets dictate? The recent religious and occult revival might make it seem that way.

But I do not think that is the case. If anything, probably the opposite is the case. For the first time ever, we are throwing the cold, clear light of science on these "superstitions" and finding out just what's true and what isn't. By actively and critically investigating these areas, we may even find principles in the workings of nature that no one ever dreamed were there.

The word *occult* is derived from the Latin for "hidden." What is now happening is that we are taking much of this previously concealed material out of hiding and exposing it to the light of day. As we do so, we are finding that it is structured systematically, just as the rest of the known universe is, though perhaps as differently from our currently accepted models as was Einsteinian physics from Newtonian. Unknown quantities that had previously been assigned to the mysterious "spiritual" world are now becoming increasingly recognized as perfectly normal extensions of the physical world. Indeed, before long we may have developed a fairly rigorous set of spiritual mechanics (as contradictory as that word combination may seem) that will separate so-called supernatural phenomena from morality, the two of which together make up what we have in the past called religion. St. Paul said, "You shall know the truth, and the truth shall set you free," and indeed it may before long. In the form of religion and the occult, we have been seeing a realm of nature through a glass darkly, but shortly we shall see it face to face, a step whose implications we cannot begin to estimate.

The unraveling of the effect of planetary cycles on human behavior is just an early stage in a large and important investigation that will doubtless revolutionize a world culture already in the throes of future shock. Far from making us the superstitious victims of fate, it will extend our influence into realms we hadn't imagined. There will be those who will simply refuse to believe any of it, just as there were whole nations in Africa that refused to believe that a man had set foot on the moon. But those who seize upon it and use it to their advantage will be way ahead of the game.

I hope that you see the knowledge in this book in this light. Use it as a tool to increase your efficiency and bring you ultimate success a little sooner. When greater knowledge comes along to modify or supplant what I have written here—as it certainly will—seize upon that and use it for even greater advantage.

Ultimately, knowledge *is* power, and it is the key to success. If you have read this book carefully and are willing to use it as an additional tool in making your way through life, then it was worth its cover price. If not, then both money and opportunity have been wasted.

We are entering a new age—ushered in by the advent of a hitherto undreamed-of technology. In that age those who choose to develop and utilize the technology first will be the leaders, and those who dawdle along behind will be the followers.

The time is now—and the choice is yours.

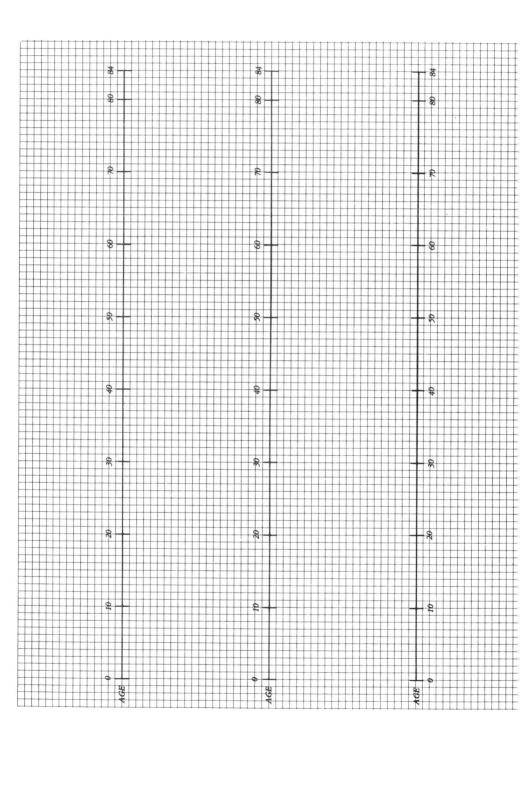

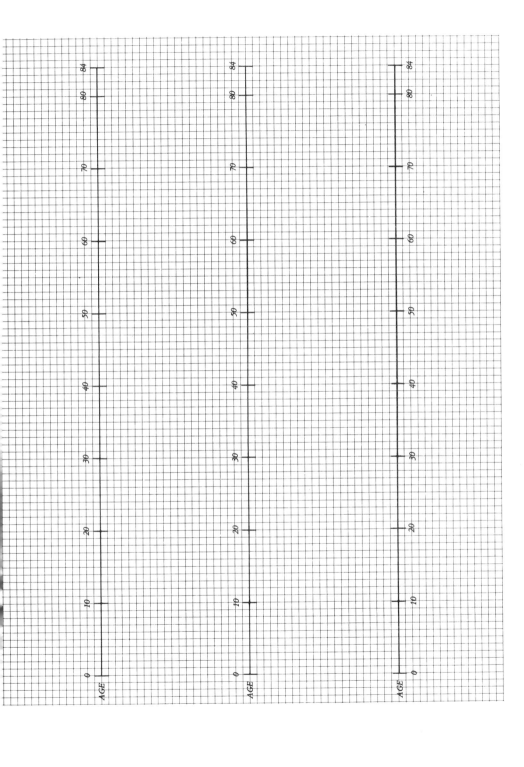

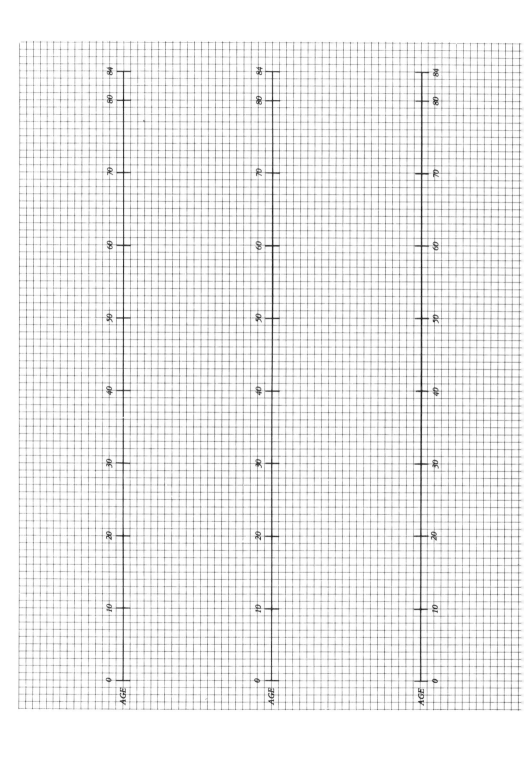

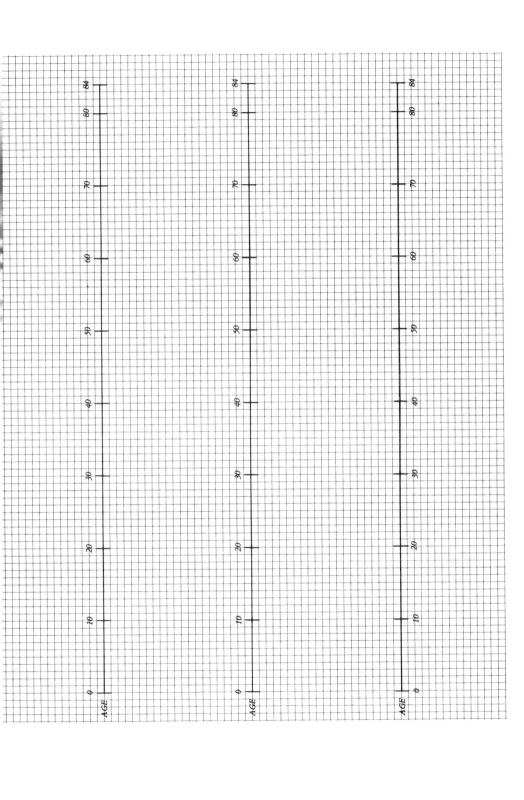

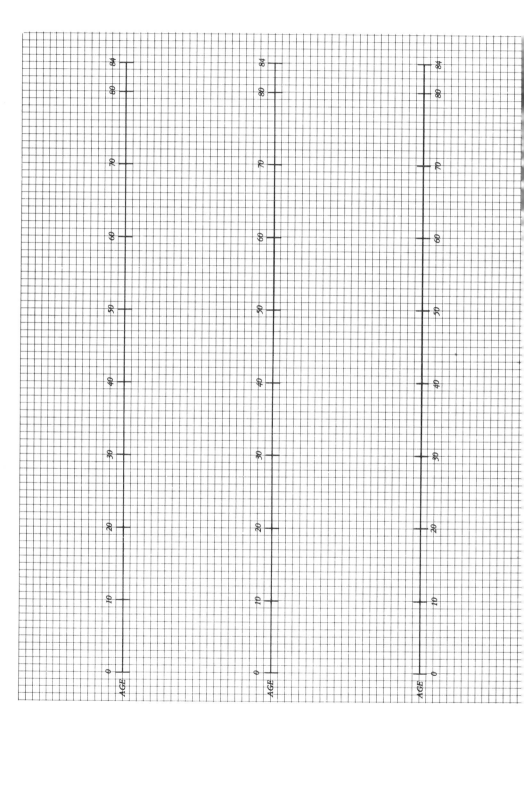

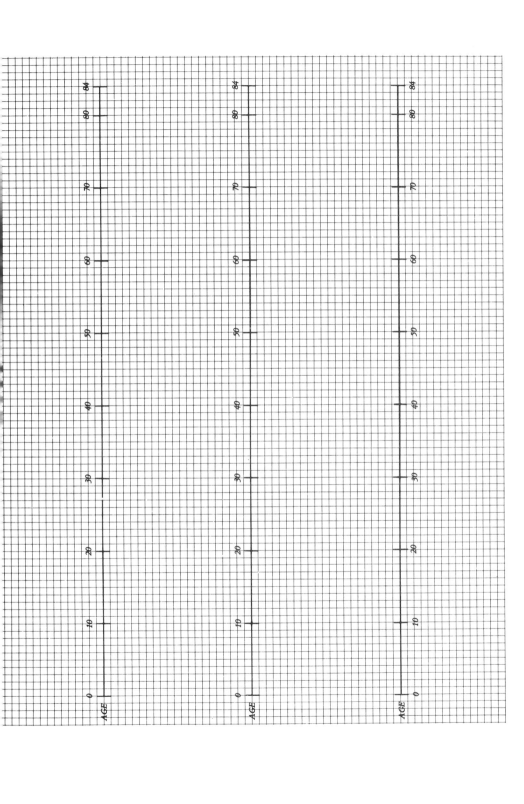

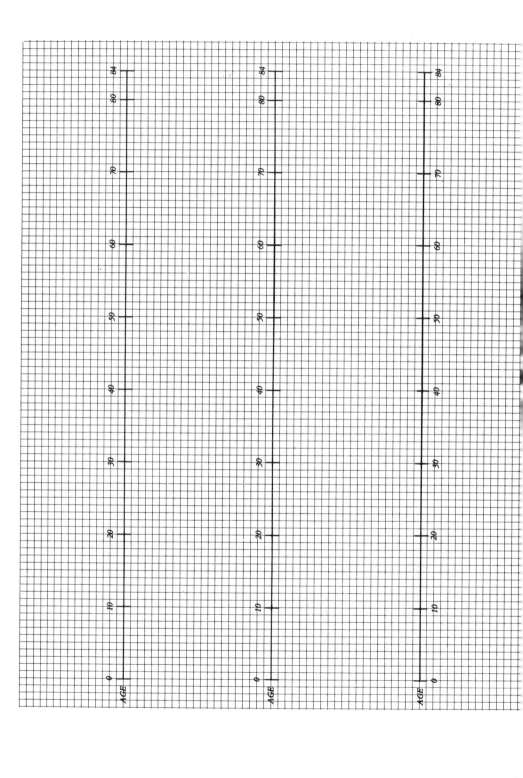